A Christian's
Wells of Joy

A Christian's Wells of Joy

By
John R. Rice, D.D., Litt. D.

Sword of the Lord Publishers
Murfreesboro, Tennessee 37130

Printed and Bound in the United States of America

TABLE OF CONTENTS

INTRODUCTION

"Ho, every one that thirsteth, come ye to the waters, and he that hath no money; come ye, buy, and eat; yea, come, buy wine and milk without money and without price."—Isa. 55:1.

What treasures of joy and blessing God has for every Christian! It is a sin for Christians not to be happy, not to be joyful. The text for the first sermon in this book is from Isaiah 12:3, "Therefore with joy shall ye draw water out of the wells of salvation." But that is a text for the whole book, too, and we trust that every reader will find new springs flowing, new rivers of blessing!

To the poor, fallen Samaritan woman Jesus offered water unlike the poor, failing, disappointing wells of this world. He said, "But whosoever drinketh of the water that I shall give him shall never thirst; but the water that I shall give him shall be in him a well of water springing up into everlasting life" (John 4:14). And in the last sweet invitation of the Bible Jesus said, "And let him that is athirst come. And whosoever will, let him take the water of life freely" (Rev. 22:17). Oh, may any hungry heart, any unsatisfied soul, any guilty sinner longing for forgiveness, drink freely today of the peace and joy and forgiveness and eternal salvation which Jesus has purchased for you and offers freely.

The Christian, Jesus said, should drink freely. "In the last day, that great day of the feast, Jesus stood and cried, saying, If any man thirst, let him come unto me, and drink. He that believeth on me, as the scripture hath said, out of his belly shall flow rivers of living water. (But this spake he of the Spirit, which they that believe on him should receive: for the Holy Ghost was not yet given; because that Jesus was not yet glorified.)" (John 7:37-39). The Christian should have that artesian well flowing out from his innermost being to all about him, the power of the Holy Spirit. And that blessed promise of the joy and power of the Holy Spirit is likened to water in Isaiah 44:3: "I will pour water upon him that is thirsty, and floods upon the dry ground: I will pour my spirit upon thy seed, and my blessing upon thine offspring."

There are wells of joy and blessing, there are answers to your problems, there is healing for your sickness, there is cleansing for your sin, there is a refreshing for the tired, weary and discouraged. Yes, there is life itself in the wells of salvation.

I beg every reader to draw water from the wells of salvation and not only have forgiveness but all the blessings offered to those who trust the Lord and follow Him.

John R. Rice
Murfreesboro, Tennessee

1971

1.

DRINK AT WELLS OF JOY!

"With joy shall ye draw water out of the wells of salvation."—Isa. 12:3.

This is a sad old world for most people. Ever since Eve came, shocked, upon the stark, cold body of her boy Abel and knew that Cain, her firstborn, her pride and joy, was the accused foul murderer, this world has been a place of tears for millions. Oh, Mother Eve, countless others will stand helpless at deathbeds and weep by the biers of the dead; countless others will find the heartbreak that comes from the perverse, fallen, wicked, deceitful heart that is back of the murders, the thefts, the adulteries, the lies, the frustrations, the crime and broken hearts of this world.

Who has joy? Not the Hollywood sex darling, Marilyn Monroe. "She had her own devil," said one movie friend. And the millions of money, the shifting from one mate to another, the drink, and the other forbidden pleasures, were unavailing and she was found naked, dead, a suicide of barbiturate excess.

Who has joy? Not the wealthy Jacqueline Kennedy Onassis, once mistress of the White House, darling of millions, but now in an adulterous marriage, spending the millions that cannot satisfy her restless heart.

Who has joy? Not the profane infidel bishop Pike who wandered from atheism to Rome, from law to the church, to an Episcopal bishopric, to a total renunciation of churches, to spiritism and quackery. His unsatisfied heart, twice divorced; his son to whom he could not even give a hope there was a hereafter, took to dope, then suicide; his secretary, disillusioned and perhaps scorned for the third wife, committed suicide. At last, Pike died wandering in the desert by the Dead Sea, seeking to "debunk" the New Testament which he despised; seeking, he said, "a historical Jesus," when he would not have the Christ of the Bible. We believe that God, tired of his blasphemy, brought Pike to judgment in a spectacular way. As far as anyone can know, he died in his sins and went to the Hell of all Christ-rejectors.

Who has joy? Not the hippies, the rebels, the demonstrators, the Civil Rights marchers, the looters, the burners, the anarchists, the Marxists. Their "trips" by marijuana or heroin or peyote or drink, their "love-ins" do not make them happy, do not give them peace and joy. "The wicked are like the troubled sea, when it cannot rest, whose waters cast up mire and dirt. There is no peace, saith my God, to the wicked" (Isa. 57:20,21).

But are not the mass of common, decent people happy? No, over a third of the marriages in America end in divorce, love is defiled, vows are broken, yea, and hearts are, too! And doubtless half of the marriages not officially broken by divorce are unhappy marriages, held together as a form only, by the children or to avoid shame, or for financial security.

When half of the girls who are married by the age of twenty are already pregnant, as some say; when fifty per cent of the women and seventy-five per cent of the men from some universities admit to pre-marital fornication—is there joy in those restless, complaining, try-anything, hearts? No, the world cannot give lasting joy!

The hundreds and hundreds of letters coming to me as editor and radio broadcaster and counseling minister, tell the sad story of frustration, of disappointment, of broken vows, broken marriages, broken friendships. They tell of guilt complexes that will not be cured, of consciences that still burn, of hopes never fulfilled. They tell of disease or disillusionment or disaster.

Oh, for the compassion of Jesus who looked upon the multitude and saw them as sheep with no shepherd. So are the people of this world!

Thank God there is another side to the picture. I know thousands of joyful Christians, with happy homes and satisfied hearts! I know singing, believing, forgiven, victorious Christians who have the joy of the Lord, with happy homes, regularly answered prayer, in their families and friends and their work. I know those who are joyful when they have to stand by open graves, joyful when they are poor, joyful when they have pain.

Oh, troubled, sinful man or woman, there is a well of salvation, a well of joy for you! Christian, you have the well; then come and draw water from it, with joy and happiness and praise!

I. SALVATION, THE WELL OF JOY!

The text quoted above in Isaiah 12:3 speaks particularly of the time when Israel will be restored to Palestine and to God, converted, saved and happy under God's daily blessing. Then, "with joy shall ye draw water from the wells of salvation," says the Scripture. But we Christians already have the well of joy, the well of salvation.

How often the Bible uses this sweet picture! We know this world is something of a dry, desert world. And in the desert, as in much of Palestine, water is the source not only of happiness but of life itself. And in this desolate world, thank God, every Christian has a well—the Water of Salvation.

When Israel, about three and one-half million strong, came out of Egypt and camped in the wilderness, in the barren sun-baked area of the Sinai Peninsula, there was no water for them. Did they, their wives and little ones, their flocks and herds, die of thirst and were their withered corpses left in that desert land? Oh, no, for Moses cried to God and we are told:

"And the Lord said unto Moses, Go on before the people, and take with thee of the elders of Israel; and thy rod, wherewith thou smotest the river, take in thine hand, and go. Behold, I will stand before thee there upon the rock in Horeb; and thou shalt smite the rock, and there shall come water out of it, that the people may drink. And Moses did so in the sight of the elders of Israel."—Exod. 17:5, 6.

When Moses had smitten that great rock with the rod of God, there poured such a river as would water all those millions of people and their livestock!

Four of us hunted elk in the Rocky Mountains just east of Yellowstone Park and north of the entrance. And up perhaps seven thousand feet high, there gushed out of the mountain daily a river of water, millions of gallons, with an unending roar. So it was in the wilderness when water came out of the rock.

But the water that flowed from the rock had meaning for us. We read in I Corinthians 10:4 that the children of Israel "drank of that spiritual Rock that followed them: and that Rock was Christ." Oh, that rock pictured the smitten, crucified Saviour! And the fountain of water which opened then pictures the everlasting life and salvation purchased for us by the death of the Saviour. And when they came again to the waters of Marah seventeen years later, Moses was instructed now only to speak to the rock, not to smite it, for when Christ died once, eternal salvation was purchased and thank God, the one who has salvation needs not to be converted again. Already he has within him the fountain and he needs only speak to Christ for the water to flow within him.

So it is that in Isaiah 55:1 the lost and troubled and thirsty are invited, "Ho, every one that thirsteth, come ye to the waters, and he that hath no money; come ye, buy, and eat; yea, come, buy wine and milk without money and without price."

So in Isaiah 44:3 God promises, "I will pour water upon him that is thirsty, and floods upon the dry ground: I will pour my spirit upon thy seed, and my blessing upon thine offspring."

Oh, God offers the well of salvation to sinners, the well of joy, the fountain of peace and blessing!

There was a Samaritan woman at Jacob's Well in Sychar when Jesus came that way. She had lived a frustrated life, had married five times, and now disillusioned, disappointed, she is living in sin with another man, unmarried. Jesus told her, ". . .Whosoever drinketh of this water shall thirst again: But whosoever drinketh of the water that I shall give him shall never thirst; but the water that I shall give him shall be in him a well of water springing up into everlasting life" (John 4:13,14).

Yes, one who takes Christ not only has a drink of water but he has planted within him an artesian well of joy and blessing, a flowing stream of salvation. And how gladly that poor, shabby, disillusioned, half-heathen woman received it!

> **Jesus gave her water that was not from the well,**
> **Gave her living water, and sent her forth to tell;**
> **She went away singing,**
> **And came back bringing**
> **Others for the water that was not from the well.**

Oh, this well of salvation is not only for the individual but for all those about him. In John 7:37-39 we find this teaching by the Saviour:

"In the last day, that great day of the feast, Jesus stood and cried, saying, If any man thirst, let him come unto me, and drink. He that believeth on me, as the scripture hath said, out of his belly shall flow rivers of living water. (But this spake he of the Spirit, which they that believe on him should receive: for the Holy Ghost was not yet given; because that Jesus was not yet glorified.)"

Not only does the Christian have a well of water for himself; it is God's plan that this artesian well, this flowing fountain, should reach out to all those about him as he gives the Gospel of salvation to others.

You see, the dear Lord wants every sinner, and the invitation is to "whosoever will"; so in the last chapter in the last book in the Bible God gives one final and blessed repetition of the sweet invitation He has worded in a thousand different ways throughout the holy pages before it: "And the Spirit and the bride say, Come. And let him that heareth say, Come. And let him that is athirst come. And whosoever will, let him take the water of life freely" (Rev. 22:17).

Oh, there is a well of joy, blessing and happiness for all who will take of the Water of Life.

II. WHAT IS IN THIS WELL OF SALVATION? WHAT ARE THE SOURCES OF CHRISTIAN JOY?

How much there is to make a Christian happy! What a wonderful fountain of joy there is in salvation! What is in this well of salvation from which we may draw with joy?

1. There Is the Joy of Sins Forgiven

I do not wonder that in naming "all his benefits," the psalmist first of all reminded his soul of the blessing that God "forgiveth all thine iniquities." Oh, sins forgiven! Conscience cleared and made easy! The fear of judgment gone! The slavery of habit and lust broken!

In Luke 10 we read how Jesus sent seventy others besides His disciples out to preach and witness in every city and town whither He would come. They were given power over unclean spirits, and power to heal the sick, and power to cast out devils. They returned with joy saying, "Lord, even the devils are subject unto us through thy name" (vs. 17). But Jesus said unto them, "Rejoice not, that the spirits are subject unto you; but rather rejoice, because your names are written in heaven" (vs. 20).

The prodigal son surely had joy when he had gone back home, when the father had received him with a kiss of forgiveness, put on him a robe of righteousness, given him a ring of sonship and the shoes of the preparation of the Gospel of peace. Sitting at the feast of the homecoming, the prodigal knew no more of the hunger and the filth and the loneliness and frustration of the hogpen and famine where he had been. Oh, the joy of salvation, forgiveness, and a home in Heaven!

2. The Christian Has a Comforter, a Friend, a Guide, a Teacher—the Holy Spirit

When He was going away, the dear Lord urged the disciples not to grieve. Rather He said they should rejoice because "I will send a Comforter unto you." He is "another Comforter," that is, One like Jesus, with a wonderful added advantage that He can live in the body of every Christian.

It would be wonderful if Jesus were on earth in a physical body now. If sometime in long travel and in the midst of some great crowd I could draw near and just look in His face for a few minutes and hear Him speak as never man spake. But how much better that I can have Christ manifested within me daily, and the Father made known to my heart through the blessed work of the indwelling Holy Spirit, the Comforter. He is the Comforter to comfort the heart and spread abroad the love of God in our hearts.

He is the Guide who guides us into all truth. He is the teacher who explains the Bible. He is the prayer-helper who prays for us with groanings that cannot be uttered and helps us pray in the will of God. Oh, the Comforter can kiss all the bruises of misfortune, explain all the doubtful questions, and make the Lord Jesus and the Father very real to us! This is part of the water of salvation which we may draw with joy.

3. What Joy That the Christian Can Seek and Have Daily Fellowship With God!

In Psalm 16:11 we read, "In thy presence is fulness of joy; at thy right hand there are pleasures for evermore." One can have conscious fellowship with the Father and with the Son. First John 1:3, 4, says, ". . .and truly our fellowship is with the Father, and with his Son Jesus Christ. And these things write we unto you, that your joy may be full." Oh, to know the Lord Jesus more intimately by daily fellowship is a joy that no unconverted person can ever have. It is yours freely, Christian. Take it!

4. The Joy of Answered Prayer

Jesus wants us to be happy. He particularly names one way for us to have this Christian joy: "Hitherto have ye asked nothing in my name: ask, and ye shall receive, that your joy may be full" (John 16:24).

Oh, the joy of answered prayer!

Years ago I was in a citywide revival campaign in Clarksburg, West Virginia. The fundamental, Bible-believing churches that sponsored the campaign were small. The faith and wisdom of those who prepared the campaign were small. We started in the great City Auditorium following the reproach of a disgraceful, so-called revival by cultists, with bribed witnesses to fake healings, etc. A thousand dollars was borrowed for the down payment on the rental on the auditorium. Oh, how we struggled to get out advertising and to build up the crowd. Little by little the crowds increased. There were nights of prayer. There was pleading before God. There was burden indescribable to reach a city calloused and indifferent, and to stir cold Christians and to reach the unsaved. Yes, and a burden, too, to meet the expenses so we could pay back borrowed money, pay the musicians, and come out with victory and a good name.

At last the windows of Heaven seemed to open. The floodtide came. Wonderful conversions of drunkards! Oh, the deep-settled conviction, the tears, the repentance, and the glad decisions! The crowds came. Soon all bills were paid, and many were saved.

On the closing night, I left my wife and secretary to meet me at the entrance. I walked down across the viaduct to get the car, which, because of the great crowds, had been parked far away from the auditorium. As I walked along in the moonlight my heart overflowed with joy. Before I knew it I said aloud, "Praise the Lord!" It was the joy of answered prayer. Again I said it, louder still, "Oh, praise the Lord!" And then louder still until I caught myself and thought, "I may get arrested! Somebody may think I am drunk!"

Oh, God has a way to happiness: praying in the will of God, getting our prayers answered and then rejoicing about it! A life of joyful answered prayer is the proper lot for every child of God.

5. The Scriptures, Wonderful Fountain of Joy!

How sweet is the Word of God to the believing heart that is tuned to hear it! "The judgments of the Lord are true and righteous altogether. More to be desired are they than gold, yea, than much fine gold: sweeter also than honey and the honeycomb" says Psalm 19:9,10.

Jeremiah too learned that sweet joy. He said, "Thy words were found, and I did eat them; and thy word was unto me the joy and rejoicing of mine heart" (Jer. 15:16).

When I was sixteen or seventeen, we lived on a stock farm in West Texas and raised fine horses. Christmastime came. All the family was invited to Grandpa Bellah's home in Decatur, Texas, for the Christmas season. But someone must milk the cows and feed the horses and look after the place. And that was my job. I had baker's bread enough. There was milk and cereal and fresh eggs and bacon and butter. And I could look after my simple needs. I would miss the Christmas tree, the fellowship, the Christmas

nner. But I was a Christian and the Bible became very
weet to me. How I reveled in it for hours during those
ays, which otherwise might have been lonely days! For
ne first time I found what sweet comfort and
nlightenment and joy could come from the Word of God.

Oh, it is foolish for a Christian to be hungry when he
ight be fed, to be sad when he might be joyful, to be in
arkness when he can have the light! What joy in the
criptures for the believing heart that loves the Bible!

6. The Special Joy of the Soul Winner

One of the highest joys any Christian may ever know is
ne joy of winning souls. Psalm 126:5 and 6 says, "They
at sow in tears shall reap in joy. He that goeth forth and
eepeth, bearing precious seed, shall doubtless come again
ith rejoicing, bringing his sheaves with him." One may
w in tears and reap in joy; one may go forth in weeping,
it he will come back rejoicing with sheaves. We learn that
hen the shepherd finds the lost sheep he "layeth it on his
oulders, rejoicing. And when he cometh home, he calleth
gether his friends and neighbours, saying unto them,
ejoice with me; for I have found my sheep which was
st" (Luke 15:5,6). Those in Heaven with the angels
joice over souls saved, and the Christian may rejoice with
sus.

When in John, chapter 4, the Lord Jesus had won the
amaritan woman and she had run away to tell others of
e wonderful happenings and to bring them to meet the
aviour and be saved, the disciples said to Jesus, "Master,
t." But He answered them, "I have meat to eat that ye
ow not of" (John 4:31,32). The meat Jesus had was
etter than any sandwiches or salad or fruit the disciples
ight offer him. By Jacob's Well in Sychar He had the joy

of seeing a soul saved.

Oh, how many times I have known that joy! It will b
the main joy when I meet the Saviour, I am sure, as it
now His principal joy.

Those who win souls are happy. They do people mor
good, they receive more love and gratitude and greate
rewards in Heaven than those who do any other goo
thing.

III. OH, CHRISTIAN, DRAW THE WATER FROM YOUR WELL OF SALVATION WITH JOY!

The text says, "With joy shall ye draw water out of th
wells of salvation." That indicates that those who have th
well of salvation still should give attention, should choos
to draw. Then, Christian, see that you have the joy that i
yours, the joy provided, in the wonderful well of salvatio
which all those who have trusted in Christ have.

How Important It Is to Have the Joy of Salvation

One who loses the joy of salvation may think that he ha
lost his salvation. It is hard to feel right when you are doin
wrong. When the blessed Holy Spirit rebukes us and ou
conscience condemns us for our sins, we are likely to fee
rejected of God. It may be as the Apostle Peter said, tha
such backslidden Christians forget that they were purge
from their old sins (II Pet. 1:9). The *assurance* of salvatio
sometimes goes with the *joy* of salvation.

But one of the marks that all the world can recognize a
fitting a Christian is that of being joyful. The dear Lor
Jesus said, "By this shall all men know that ye are m
disciples, if ye have love one to another" (John 13:35). Bu
I think that we may also say that it is wholly out of plac

for a Christian to be defeated, to be disconsolate, to be worried, fretted and unhappy. A Christian has much to rejoice at, and surely the lost world about him will not be much impressed with what Christ can do if He does not satisfy the hungry heart and give joy to the troubled. You are a poor testimony for Christ if you are not a joyful, happy Christian.

One's strength in Christian work depends largely on his joy. When the remnant of Jews returned to Jerusalem to rebuild the walls under Nehemiah, they became conscious of their sins and failures and they were heartsick. They would have mourned, but Nehemiah told them that they should rejoice in the Lord, should send gifts to others, should celebrate God's blessings for "the joy of the Lord is your strength." Proverbs 17:22 tells us, "A merry heart doeth good like a medicine." Not only will your health be better, your rest sweeter, your food more tasty, your face more pleasant; but you will work better, you will be more sure of God's leading, you will be more confident of blessing, if you have the joy of the Lord.

It is important for Christians to be happy. How it dishonors God for one upon whom God has poured such blessings, and to whom He has made such promises, and to whom He has given such a wonderful Saviour and salvation, not to be happy!

What Things May Cause a Christian to Lose His Joy?

Surely sin can cause a Christian to lose his joy. When from his palace rooftop, David gazed on the naked Bathsheba in the night and when he played with lust and had her come to meet him in the palace, and then led her into sin, then had her husband murdered to try to cover his sin, David lost his joy. The pitiful prayer and cry of Psalm 51 tells us how he could say, "My sin is ever before me." The guilt, the self-reproach, the public disgrace, the curse on his children—all these resulting from sin—took away David's joy. So he prayed, "Restore unto me the joy of thy salvation" (Ps. 51:12). He still had the salvation, but he had lost the joy of it.

Oh, a burning conscience takes away the joy of salvation! A sense of God's displeasure and the certainty of punishment may ruin all the Christian's joy.

But sometimes it is not a gross, vulgar, flagrant sin that suddenly sweeps away the Christian's joy. Rather, it may be preoccupation, becoming burdened about many matters. This may cause one to neglect the place of prayer and to neglect the sweetness of the Scripture, to neglect even the conscious fellowship of God until his joy is gone.

In the parable of the sower, when some of the good seed was sowed among the thorns, "the thorns sprang up with it, and choked it. . .And that which fell among thorns are they, which, when they have heard, go forth, and are choked with cares and riches and pleasures of this life, and bring no fruit to perfection" (Luke 8:7,14).

A water faucet was found to be of no use. When the faucet was turned on, it gave no water. At last a dead rat was found that had clogged the pipe, defiled and stopped the water. So it is sometimes with flagrant, gross sin.

But some other time there may be a slow accretion of a little sand or dirt which little by little reduces the flow until it is but a trickle. So by lack of attention and being preoccupied with many burdens or pleasures or of a business or with other people, one may lose the joy of the Lord.

3. How Then Is One to Restore the Joy and Be Happy?

We remember that David "encouraged himself in the Lord" in a great time of grief and trouble when Ziklag was burned and his family and those of his soldiers were captured by the Amalekites (I Sam. 30:6). And so a Christian may set out to restore his joy. Troubled on every side, the psalmist cried out to himself, "Why art thou cast down, O my soul? and why art thou disquieted within me? hope thou in God: for I shall yet praise him, who is the health of my countenance, and my God." How sweet is that verse which is quoted, with only a word or two of variation, three times in Psalm 42 and once in Psalm 43.

Oh, a Christian has the duty and privilege of seeking and having the joy of the Lord restored. He need not be cast down, need not be fretted, need not be sad, need not feel guilty nor fear failure.

How may one restore his joy? First, of course, confess and forsake sin. So David did in the 51st Psalm, and in that very matter he asked for the restoration of the joy of salvation. And "if we confess our sins, he is faithful and just to forgive us our sins, and to cleanse us from all unrighteousness" says I John 1:9.

Oh, do not hound yourself with sins of the past! If you confess them to the Lord, then take and claim the forgiveness He has promised.

A sad letter this week tells of a woman who, years ago, had an illegitimate baby. Now for years she has had some ill health and always the haunting thought that maybe God's curse is upon her and maybe. He continues to chastise her for that sin. So her question is, Can she have any forgiveness for that sin? I told her, as I tell every troubled soul who reads this, when you honestly confess a sin to God and turn your heart away from it in penitence, then you are commanded to accept the forgiveness and the cleansing and to believe it. Drop the matter and do not torment yourself with a thing already put under the blood, and do not dishonor God by doubting His sweet promise of forgiveness!

And perhaps one of the sweetest and quickest ways to get the joy of the Lord is in praise to God. Oh, count your blessings! name them one by one, and it will surprise you what the Lord hath done.

David was rejoicing when he said, "Bless the Lord, O my soul: and all that is within me, bless his holy name. Bless the Lord, O my soul, and forget not all his benefits" (Ps. 103:1,2). One who stops to praise God and counts over the good things God has given him can surely be happy.

Psalm 68:19 says that God "daily loadeth us with benefits." Is there no thankfulness in your heart?

We are plainly commanded, "In every thing give thanks: for this is the will of God in Christ Jesus concerning you" (I Thess. 5:18).

Praise is due to God. It is proper and right that He should have the glad acknowledgment of His goodness. And our own happiness and our sense of approval with God will depend largely on whether or not we have a praiseful heart, a thankful heart for God's blessings.

Here is a strange way, it will seem, to have the joy of the Lord. The Lord Jesus said, "Blessed are ye, when men shall revile you, and persecute you, and shall say all manner of evil against you falsely, for my sake. Rejoice, and be exceeding glad: for great is your reward in heaven: for so persecuted they the prophets which were before you" (Matt. 5:11,12). Rejoice in persecution for Christ.

Oh, since all the things that God sends are for our

blessing, and since "all things work together for good to them that love God, to them who are the called according to his purpose," then surely the Christian can be happy in any circumstances. With his thorn in the flesh Paul could say, "Therefore I take pleasure in infirmities, in reproaches, in necessities, in persecutions, in distresses for Christ's sake: for when I am weak, then am I strong" (II Cor. 12:10). The Christian can obey the injunction to "glory in tribulation" —Rom. 5:3; see also II Cor. 7:4, "Joyful in all our tribulation!"). No circumstances, no burdens, no sorrows, no losses, no frustrations may come to a Christian if he abides in Christ and counts his blessings and confesses and forsakes his faults and seeks the Lord. The Christian may have the joy of the Lord. Oh, then, draw water from the wells of salvation!

IV. DEAR LOST SINNER, DRINK OF THIS WATER AND HAVE YOUR OWN ARTESIAN WELL!

It was to a lost woman that Jesus said, "Whosoever drinketh of this water shall thirst again: But whosoever drinketh of the water that I shall give him shall never thirst; but the water that I shall give him shall be in him a well of water springing up into everlasting life" (John 4:13,14).

It was to lost people that the Lord cried out in Isaiah 55:1, "Ho, every one that thirsteth, come ye to the waters, and he that hath no money; come ye, buy, and eat; yea, come. . . ."

And unto all the lost and troubled people in the world the last invitation in the Bible offers: "The Spirit and the bride say, Come. And let him that heareth say, Come. And let him that is athirst come. And whosoever will, let him take the water of life freely" (Rev. 22:17).

Oh, you may have your own well within you and from that you may draw with joy the waters of salvation all your days and rejoice forever with Christ in Heaven.

Are you tired of the disappointment? the disillusionment? the failures? the sin of the old life? Then turn to Jesus for forgiveness and drink of this Water of Life today!

If you will here and now admit yourself to be a poor, lost sinner who needs salvation, if you will honestly face the fact that all these other things do not satisfy you, you may be saved here and now.

> **The world deceives me;**
> > **It offers peace and joy and rest,**
> **But ever leaves me**
> > **With hungry heart and second best;**
> **I came to Jesus,**
> > **And there I found it all I'd missed!**
>
> **His yoke is easy**
> > **His burden light;**
> **His way is happy**
> > **and always bright.**
> **In this world's midnight,**
> > **He is my light.**
> **His yoke is easy,**
> > **His burden light.**

If you are ready to turn your heart from sin and put your trust in Jesus, remember that He offers salvation free. Your sins are all paid for on the cross. Now by simply trusting Jesus Christ to forgive and save, you may have everlasting life and your own well of joy.

Can you honestly say yes to God and choose to drink today? Then, I beg you first, decide it in your heart and then sign the decision form below, copy it in a letter and mail it to me.

Evangelist John R. Rice
P. O. Box 1099
Murfreesboro, Tennessee 37130

Dear Brother Rice:

I have read your sermon on "Drink at Wells of Joy." I admit I am a poor, lost sinner. I have found this world does not give happiness. I have found that Satan's promises do not turn out well. I know I need forgiveness. I want the peace and joy that God can give a forgiven soul. I want to know I am going to Heaven.

So here and now I confess that I am a sinner, I turn to Jesus Christ to forgive me. I will take Him now as my Saviour, trusting Him. I will claim Him and will set out to live for Him. I rely on Him to take me to Heaven in His time.

Now that I am taking Christ as my own personal Saviour, will you write me a letter of encouragement and counsel as to how to live for God?

Signed ——————————————————————————

Address ——————————————————————————

———————————————————————————————

2.
JOY FROM THE WELL OF PRAYER

"O thou that hearest prayer, unto thee shall all flesh come."—Ps. 65:2.

I. GOD HEARS PRAYER

Among the many, many titles and names of our wonderful Lord in the Bible is this divine title also, "Thou that hearest prayer."

It is the distinction of great men of God that they prayed. It is the distinction of our God that He answers prayer. Answered prayer binds together the true God and His true believers in the minds of people of the whole world.

Abraham was a man who prayed, and Abraham's God was the God who answered prayer. So Abraham's servant, starting after a bride for Isaac, prayed, "O Lord God of my master Abraham, I pray thee, send me good speed this day, and shew kindness unto my master Abraham" (Gen. 24:12).

When God would identify Himself to His people as the God who reveals Himself to men, the God who answers prayer, He spoke of Himself as the God of Abraham, and the God of Isaac, and the God of Jacob. To Jacob, He said in Genesis 28:13, "I am the Lord God of Abraham thy father, and the God of Isaac." When God revealed Himself to Moses in the wilderness, He revealed Himself as the God who answered the prayers of Abraham, Isaac and Jacob (Exod. 3:16).

Elijah on Mount Carmel needed a God who could answer prayer. The prophets of Baal had called in vain on their god and he did not answer. So Elijah prayed to the "Lord God of Abraham, Isaac, and of Israel" that He would answer by fire from Heaven (I Kings 18:36).

Elijah got his prayer answered. Ravens from Heaven fed him. The widow's oil and meal were multiplied. The widow's son was raised to life. God answered his prayer with fire from Heaven. When he and Elisha came to the Jordan River and Elijah smote the water with his mantle, God opened a dry path through the water and they went through. When Elisha came to ask for a miraculous manifestation of God's power at the same River Jordan, he smote the water with Elijah's mantle and said. "Where is the Lord God of Elijah?" (II Kings 2:14). The God of Elijah still lived and still answered prayer, and He did the same thing for Elisha.

How many, many times God had answered the prayer of David before Psalm 65 was written. God must have put it in the heart of David to remember when He had heard a boy cry and helped David kill the lion and the bear. God had answered prayer and a smooth stone from a sling had killed the giant Goliath. God had answered prayer and saved David from the anger of King Saul. God had answered prayer and spared David from the rebellion of Absalom. God had heard prayer and had forgiven his wicked sin with Bathsheba. God had heard prayer and stopped the plague of Jerusalem when thousands were dying. So God inspired David to write in Psalm 65:2, "O thou that hearest prayer, unto thee shall all flesh come."

Personal God Proven by Revealed Word, by Incarnation, by Answered Prayer

The reality of God is proved in His revelation to men. This revelation comes to us first in the Bible. We have a living God, a personal God, a real God, who has made His will known to us in the Bible. The Bible, verbally inspired, absolutely reliable and infallible, proves itself to be of God and thereby proves a real God.

Next, God is proved in the incarnation of Christ. Christ is God: "He that hath seen me hath seen the Father." The very fact of a real Jesus proves a real and personal God. The mercy and gentleness of Jesus proves the mercy of God. His death on the cross proves both the love of God for sinners and the wrath of God on sin. God is revealed in His Son as well as in the Bible.

But third, God reveals Himself to individuals in personal experience by answering their prayers. I know there is a God, not only because of the Bible and not only because of a historically proved Christ, but I know there is a real and personal God because He has answered MY prayers. He saved my soul when I called upon Him. He gave me peace when I was in trouble. He gave me assurance in answer to prayer when I had doubted. He gave me money to go through school. He raised my father from what appeared to be a deathbed, in answer to prayer. He has given great revivals in answer to prayer, contrary to the plans and expectations of men. And now for many years He has provided food, clothing, and every financial need for me and my family, without any set salary or any promised, definite income from any source in the world. I say that personal experience of answered prayer proves there is a God.

Answering prayer is one of the attributes of God, as much a part of the nature of God as His holiness or His omnipotence. Since God is what He is, He must be a prayer-hearing God.

Prayer Changes Things

For God to hear a prayer means that prayer must change things. Prayer, as used in the Bible, does not refer simply to a worshipful attitude nor simply to an attitude of praise and meditation. Prayer, in the Bible, means asking God for something. Jesus said,

"Ask, and it shall be given you; seek, and ye shall find; knock, and it shall be opened unto you: For every one that asketh receiveth; and he that seeketh findeth; and to him that knocketh it shall be opened."—Matt. 7:7,8.

Prayer, in the Bible, is asking, knocking, seeking. Again the Saviour told His disciples, "Hitherto have ye asked nothing in my name: ask, and ye shall receive, that your joy may be full" (John 16:24).

James 4:2 says, "Ye have not, because ye ask not." Jesus said that if we, being evil, know how to give good gifts to our children, how much more would the heavenly Father give good things to them that ASK Him? When the disciples begged Jesus, "Lord, teach us to pray," He taught them to say, "Give us this day our daily bread"—a definite request for a material answer that very day. Evidently one should pray after this manner every day. I say, prayer, in the Bible, is definitely asking God to do something that otherwise we would not expect Him to do. Prayer, in the Bible sense, means to get God to change things. Prayer does change things.

The Bible clearly teaches that prayer changes even the plans of God. If that seems shocking to you, remember the prayer of King Hezekiah. God had said to him, "Set thine house in order: for thou shalt die, and not live." But when

Hezekiah turned his face to the wall, wept and prayed, God changed His plan before the prophet had gotten out the front gate, and sent Isaiah back to say, "I have heard thy prayer, I have seen thy tears: behold, I will add unto thy days fifteen years" (Isa. 38:1-5). God had planned for Hezekiah to die at once but changed His plans in answer to prayer. Hezekiah lived fifteen years longer than he would have lived had he not prayed! Prayer, I must insist, can change even the plan of God.

God sent Jonah to preach to Nineveh, "Forty days, and Nineveh shall be overthrown" (Jonah 3:4), but when the people repented in sackcloth and ashes, with fasting, we are told, "And God saw their works, that they turned from their evil way; and God repented of the evil, that he had said that he would do unto them; and he did it not" (Jonah 3:10). The prayer of the Ninevites changed the plan of God and He did not do that which He had said He would do to them.

When Moses was on Mount Sinai, the Israelites were naked, dancing wildly about the golden calf Aaron had made. God told Moses about it and said, "Now therefore let me alone, that my wrath may wax hot against them, and that I may consume them: and I will make of thee a great nation" (Exod. 32:10). But Moses prayed with all his heart and then we are told, "The Lord repented of the evil which he thought to do unto his people" (Exod. 32:9-14). The intercession of Moses kept God from destroying Israel.

Praying changes things, changes even the plan of God. This is a clear teaching of the Word of God.

II. ELIJAH'S WELL IS FOR US TOO

"Elias was a man subject to like passions as we are, and he prayed."—James 5:17.

Elijah's God Still Answers Prayer the Same Today

God hears prayer! God hears prayer today the same as in the days of Elijah. The Bible is full of encouragement for Christians to pray, to pray big prayers, to a great God, expecting mighty answers.

When the time came for Elijah to go to Heaven, the world faced the loss of the one man then living, as far as was publicly known, who could shake Heaven with his prayers. Would miracles cease? Would the wondrous works which God had done through Elijah and in answer to his prayers, never be seen again? The scores of the "sons of the prophets" were all apparently agreed that with the passing of Elijah, wonderful answers to prayer would cease. That is, all seemed agreed but one man. Elisha, the son of Shaphat, who "poured water on the hands of Elijah" (II Kings 3:11), believed in the unchanging God, the God who answers the prayer of faith in all generations.

"And it came to pass, when the Lord would take up Elijah into heaven by a whirlwind, that Elijah went to Elisha from Gilgal. And Elijah said unto Elisha, Tarry here, I pray thee; for the Lord hath sent me to Bethel. And Elisha said unto him, As the Lord liveth, and as thy soul liveth, I will not leave thee. So they went down to Bethel. And the sons of the prophets that were at Bethel came forth to Elijah, and said unto him, Knowest thou that the Lord will take away thy master from thy head today? And he said, Yea, I know it; hold ye your peace. And Elijah said unto him, Elisha, tarry here, I pray thee; for the Lord hath sent me to Jericho. And he said, As the Lord liveth, and as thy soul liveth, I will not leave thee. So they came to Jericho. And the sons of the prophets that were at Jericho came to Elisha, and said unto him, Knowest thou that the Lord will take away thy master from thy head to day? And

he answered, Yea, I know it; hold ye your peace. And Elijah said unto him, Tarry, I pray thee, here; for the Lord hath sent me to Jordan. And he said, As the Lord liveth, and as thy soul liveth, I will not leave thee. And they two went on. And fifty men of the sons of the prophets went, and stood to view afar off: and they two stood by Jordan. And Elijah took his mantle, and wrapped it together, and smote the waters, and they were divided hither and thither, so that they two went over on dry ground. And it came to pass, when they were gone over, that Elijah said unto Elisha, Ask what I shall do for thee, before I be taken away from thee. And Elisha said, I pray thee, let a double portion of thy spirit be upon me. And he said, Thou hast asked a hard thing: nevertheless, if thou see me when I am taken from thee, it shall be so unto thee; but if not, it shall not be so. And it came to pass, as they still went on, and talked, that, behold, there appeared a chariot of fire, and horses of fire, and parted them both asunder; and Elijah went up by a whirlwind into heaven. And Elisha saw it, and he cried, My father, my father, the chariot of Israel, and the horsemen thereof. And he saw him no more: and he took hold of his own clothes, and rent them into pieces. He took up also the mantle of Elijah that fell from him, and went back, and stood by the bank of Jordan; And he took the mantle of Elijah that fell from him, and smote the waters, and said, Where is the Lord God of Elijah? and when he also had smitten the waters, they parted hither and thither: and Elisha went over.''—II Kings 2:1-14.

On the day Elijah was to be taken to Heaven, that forthcoming event was known to all, but only Elisha determined to be with the old prophet to the last, to receive his mantle and have a double portion of his spirit. He disregarded the sons of the prophets and even the suggestions of Elijah himself, and followed Elijah from

Gilgal to Bethel, from Bethel to Jericho, from Jericho to the Jordan; and when Elijah wrapped his mantle together and smote the waters so that they were divided, Elisha walked with Elijah on dry ground through the river bed and made the final request: "I pray thee, let a double portion of thy spirit be upon me."

That was one of the most audacious prayers any man ever prayed! No wonder Elijah said, "Thou hast asked a hard thing." But Elisha met the conditions, stayed with the prophet until he was taken to Heaven in a whirlwind accompanied by a chariot of fire, and picked up the mantle of Elijah as it fell.

He immediately assumed that God had heard his prayer and so Elisha demanded a miracle from God. Verses 13 and 14 of the passage above tell us that "He took up also the mantle of Elijah that fell from him, and went back, and stood by the bank of Jordan; And he took the mantle of Elijah that fell from him, and smote the waters, and said, Where is the Lord God of Elijah? and when he also had smitten the waters, they parted hither and thither: and Elisha went over."

Where is the Lord God of Elijah? That question comes ringing down through the years—sometimes uttered as a prayer of faith—asking God to show His power. Other times it is the doubting cry of one who wonders if God has ceased to answer prayer as He once did. But thank God, the Bible does not leave the question here, and we have positive, repeated proof throughout the Bible that God answers prayers the same in every age.

New Testament Makes Elijah Our Model in Prayer

Elisha not only had prayers answered as well as Elijah,

he asked for and got "a double portion" of the Spirit of
Elijah. The recorded miracles by the hand of Elisha are
double that of his master! God honored his faith when
others had no faith. The God of Elijah was also the God of
Elisha.

But happily, we find explicitly in the New Testament
that Elijah ought to be our model in prayer as he was the
model of his servant Elisha. In James 5:16-18 we read:

*"Confess your faults one to another, and pray one for
another, that ye may be healed. The effectual fervent
prayer of a righteous man availeth much. Elias was a man
subject to like passions as we are, and he prayed earnestly
that it might not rain: and it rained not on the earth by the
space of three years and six months. And he prayed again,
and the heaven gave rain, and the earth brought forth her
fruit."*

Here we are taught that Elijah (Elias sometimes in the
New Testament) was a man like we are, subject to the
same weaknesses and passions as we are. We are
encouraged to pray like Elijah prayed and expect answers
like he got from God. With Elijah and his prayers as a
model, we are commanded to pray "one for another" and
we are told that "the effectual fervent prayer of a righteous
man availeth much." The Lord clearly intended us to
believe that the prayer of a righteous man avails as much
today as it did in the days of Elijah.

The God Who Hears Prayer

God loves to be known as the God who hears prayer. He
taught the psalmist to approach Him with the divinely
inspired title, "O thou that hearest prayer" (Ps. 65:2).
That is one of the precious names He chooses and He is

pleased for men to call Him by that name. He should like to have a reputation among men as the One who hears prayer! We are told that "without faith it is impossible to please him," and that being true, we may be sure that God is more pleased by the prayer of great faith than the prayer of little faith.

The spiritually minded Bible reader cannot help seeing how the Lord was delighted when challenged by the big prayers of the Bible. How He seems to have delighted at the challenge of Moses to open and cross the Red Sea at the wave of a rod; at the request of Hezekiah for lengthened life; for the destruction of Sennacherib's army. Certainly God used men in the Bible far beyond what they deserved. For instance, Samson said very little to get the marvelous power of God except to expect it. Expecting great things from God is the way to get them. God is honored and pleased when we regard Him as the God who answers prayer.

So throughout the Bible God brings us example after example of men who prayed and got the answer, and then God tells us, "These men were ordinary men, frail men, sinful men, and yet by faith, righteous men. They were men of like passions as we are, but they prayed and their prayers were answered. Therefore, dear frail Christian, take heart and ask great things from God."

The Unchanging God

We are encouraged to pray by the fact that God never changes. Speaking to a disobedient and rebellious Israel, God said in Malachi 3:6, "For I am the Lord, I change not; therefore ye sons of Jacob are not consumed."

Even the rebellion of Israel and her many sins could not change the God of mercy, the God who answers prayer! As he Father is, so is the Son. "Jesus Christ the same yesterday, and today, and forever" (Heb. 13:8).

This unchanging God has sometimes dealt with men by dispensations. I mean that before the coming of Christ there were ceremonies and sacrifices which have now been fulfilled in the coming of the Saviour, the Lamb of God. There were ceremonial laws which have been nailed to the cross of Christ. The law is a schoolmaster to bring men to Christ.

But I remind you that there are no dispensational changes in the matter of prayer. God is a prayer-hearing God just as He is our all-powerful God, a righteous God. Prayer-hearing is an element in the very nature of the unchanging God. "O thou that hearest prayer" is an unchanging title of an unchanging God. As God's mercy has gone out to sinners in all ages and dispensations, and under all covenants, so in all ages God has heard prayer. When you study the prayers of Abraham, of Moses, of David, of Elijah, of Hezekiah, of the New Testament apostles, you can find no difference in the spirit nor in the way God answered when they cried in faith for mighty answers. In the matter of prayer, God is an unchanging God.

That is the reason God constantly reminds us of how He has answered the prayers of others. Here in James 5:16-18 we are reminded that God heard Elijah pray; therefore we should pray. In Psalm 81:10 we are told, "I am the Lord thy God, which brought thee out of the land of Egypt; open thy mouth wide, and I will fill it." Here God reminds His people in every age of His wonderful works as He brought the children of Israel out of the land of Egypt. He reminds us that He is the God who sent plagues on Egypt, plagues of blood, frogs, lice, hail, disease, boils, rain, locust and darkness, then the supernatural death of every Egyptian first-born! He is the same God who opened the Red Sea, then closed it; who destroyed Pharaoh and his entire army. He is the God of the pillar of cloud and fire, the God of the manna from Heaven, the God who brought water from the rock, the God who sustained the nation so that the Israelites' clothes waxed not old for forty years! He is the God who spoke from Mount Sinai, a miracle-working, prayer-hearing God. Therefore, God entreats us, "OPEN THY MOUTH WIDE, AND I WILL FILL IT."

God pleads with us to remember His marvelous works and to give Him a chance to prove Himself to us again. We are not to ask small things only but we are to open our mouths wide enough to receive great things from God. All this is on the clear teaching that the God of today deals with men on the prayer matter just as He did in the days when He brought Israel out of Egypt's bondage.

Jeremiah lived in the days of declension, apostasy, sin and judgment. God seemed to have hid His face from Israel, and Jeremiah saw them carried away into captivity. Jeremiah cried, 'There is no sorrow like unto my sorrow' (Lam. 1:12). Perhaps we would think that Jeremiah was justified in saying, as some moderns do, that "the age of miracles is past." In times of distress and sorrow, we are tempted to believe that our case is too hard for God, or that God does not answer prayer for us as He did for others. But in Jeremiah 32:27 we are told that the Word of the Lord came to Jeremiah, saying, "Behold, I am the Lord, the God of all flesh: is there any thing too hard for me?" In the matter of prayer, God is the God of all flesh, and there is nothing too hard for Him.

As regards circumcision and the ceremonial law, God is the God of Israel. But as regards prayer, He is the God of all flesh! As regards Christ's offer to establish the kingdom of Heaven, as the Son of David He could say, "I am not sent but unto the lost sheep of the house of Israel" (Matt. 15:24). But when the Syrophenician woman, a Gentile, prayed the prayer of faith, then all boundaries disappeared and the same hour He healed her daughter. God makes distinctions between Jew and Gentile and between one dispensation and another in some things; but in the matter of prayer, praise His name, He is "the God of all flesh" and as much our God as the God of Abraham, Isaac, Jacob, Moses, and Elijah!

Examples Encourage Us to Pray

Someone has said that one example is worth a thousand arguments. The Bible has plenty of arguments, commands and precepts that we should pray, but happily it also has many examples.

Knowing the prevailing sin of unbelief, God gives the example of Elijah who prayed and God heard. And throughout the Bible we find that God encouraged other people to pray by reminding them of how He had heard the cries of others. To Jacob, sleeping at Bethel with a stone for a pillow, God appeared and said, "I am the Lord God of Abraham thy father, and the God of Isaac: the land whereon thou lieth, to thee will I give it, and to thy seed; . . .And, behold, I am with thee, and will keep thee in all places whither thou goest, and will bring thee again into this land; for I will not leave thee, until I have done that which I have spoken to thee of" (Gen. 28:13, 15). The God who cared for Abraham and for Isaac would care for Jacob, and with this comforting assurance Jacob believed God. When God appeared to Moses in the burning bush in the wilderness, He said to him, "I am the God of thy father, the God of Abraham, the God of Isaac, and the God of Jacob" (Exod. 3:6). In the matter of prayer, God does not change, and He is as willing to be the God of Moses and work wonders for Moses as He is for Abraham!

When Moses died, who could fill his place? What mighty things God did through Moses and for Moses when he prayed! But God appeared to Joshua and said to him,

"Moses my servant is dead; now therefore arise, go over this Jordan, thou, and all this people, unto the land which I do give to them, even to the children of Israel. Every place that the sole of your foot shall tread upon, that have I given unto you, as I said unto Moses. From the wilderness and this Lebanon even unto the great river, the river Euphrates, all the land of the Hittites, and unto the great sea toward the going down of the sun, shall be your coast. There shall not any man be able to stand before thee all the days of thy life: as I was with Moses, so I will be with thee: I will not fail thee, nor forsake thee."—Josh. 1:2-5.

The age of answered prayer, the age of blessing, did not pass when Moses died. "As I was with Moses, so I will be with thee" is the promise of God. Would God we would be encouraged to pray and expect great answers by the repeated assurance of God, that He is the unchanging God who answers prayer the same in all generations.

When the angel of the Lord appeared to Gideon to call him to deliver Israel from the Midianites in the days of the judges, we are told in Judges 6:13 that Gideon said, "Oh my Lord, if the Lord be with us, why then is all this befallen us? and where be all his miracles which our fathers told us of, saying, Did not the Lord bring us up from Egypt? but now the Lord hath forsaken us, and delivered us into the hands of the Midianites." Gideon wanted to know where the miracles were that the God of his fathers had worked. Evidently Gideon's request pleased God, for miracle after miracle was worked before his eyes. The God who brought Israel out of Egypt still lived in Gideon's day.

What I am saying is that God has always used the examples of others who prayed and whose prayers were answered as an encouragement to us to pray. So here in James 5:16-18 He selects Elijah, the mighty man of prayer, and reminds us that he was as frail as we and that God will hear our prayers as He heard the prayers of Elijah.

This Promise Given Particularly for the Last Days

Critics and scoffers are forever trying to show that the Bible is out of date. It is a favorite device of the Devil to deceive people and make them believe that God does not now deal with men as He once did. Good men are sometimes persuaded that this passage in James was only for Jews and during the age of the apostles, not for the present time at all! But the Word of God is loaded for just such criticism. And in this chapter we have unmistakable evidence that God meant it not only for this age but for the very closing days of this age.

In this same fifth chapter of James, verse 3 says to the rich men, "Ye have heaped treasure together for the last days."

Verse 7 says, "Be patient therefore, brethren, unto the coming of the Lord."

Verse 8 says, "Be ye also patient; stablish your hearts: for the coming of the Lord draweth nigh."

And verse 9 says, "Behold, the judge standeth before the door."

This fifth chapter of James is for "the last days." It is good "unto the coming of the Lord." It is for all of those who live when "the coming of the Lord draweth nigh." The injunctions and teachings of this chapter are good even when the Righteous Judge, the Lord Jesus Christ, "standeth before the door." It would be not only foolish but wicked to say that the teaching here about prayer—prayer for the sick, prayer about anything else, prayer like Elijah's—is not for us today. The context plainly shows that for us who live now, even if it is in the last days, Elijah is the model for prayer and that God who heard Elijah will also hear today the effectual fervent prayer of a righteous man, even though he be subject to the like passions of Elijah and other men.

Prayer About Healing Is Particularly Encouraged Today

The passage which we have been discussing, James 5:16-18, begins with the command, "Confess your faults one to another, and pray one for another, that ye may be healed." The healing mentioned here is literal, bodily healing, for verses 14 and 15 just before this say,

"Is any sick among you? let him call for the elders of the church; and let them pray over him, anointing him with oil in the name of the Lord: And the prayer of faith shall save the sick, and the Lord shall raise him up; and if he have committed sins, they shall be forgiven him."

Then we must conclude that the entire passage on prayer, using Elijah as a model, is intended to encourage us to pray, particularly to pray for healing of the sick. "The prayer of faith shall save the sick." And remember that we are told in the same chapter that this message is "for the last days" when "the coming of the Lord draweth nigh." God has not changed in the matter of answering prayer, and God has not changed in His disposition to heal the sick in answer to prayer.

Healing and Forgiveness Are Connected

This passage connects healing of the body and forgiveness of sins. Verse 15 tells us that "the prayer of faith shall save the sick, and the Lord shall raise him up; AND IF HE HAVE COMMITTED SINS, THEY SHALL BE FORGIVEN HIM." And verse 16 tells us that confession of sin should go with prayer and healing. That is not surprising when you remember that Isaiah 53:5 puts in the same verse that "he was wounded for our transgressions" and that "with his stripes we are healed." And then Isaiah 53:4 tells us that Jesus "hath borne our griefs, and carried our sorrows." That verse concerning the atonement of Christ is quoted in the New Testament to mean, "Himself took our infirmities, and bare our sickness." Matthew 8:16 and 17 tell us that Jesus "cast out the spirits with his word, and healed all that were sick: That it might be fulfilled which was spoken by Esaias the prophet, saying, Himself took our infirmities, and bare our sicknesses." There is a very close connection between healing of the body and forgiveness of sins. Sin in every age brings sickness. In every age the God who forgives sins, answers prayer for the sick, answers big prayers like Elijah's.

Answering prayer is as much a part of the nature of God as is His merciful attitude of forgiveness of sins. When the man sick of the palsy had his sins forgiven, Jesus then healed him as an outward evidence of inward pardon (See Mark 2).

We must not put salvation and healing on the same basis in some respects. Salvation is for every sinner who will take it, but that is not always true about healing. It is always God's will to save but not always God's will to heal. It is appointed unto men, saved and unsaved, to die the first death, with the exception of Enoch and Elijah and the saints alive at the time of the rapture. But it is not God's will for any man to die the second death, and all may escape it by simple faith in Christ.

God may not always give faith for healing. He did not remove Paul's thorn in the flesh nor the weakness of Timothy's stomach, but He will give saving faith and salvation to every sinner who asks for it, for "whosoever shall call upon the name of the Lord shall be saved."

Likewise, salvation is eternal, and "He that believeth on the Son hath everlasting life" (John 3:36). But when God answers prayer and heals the sick, in the course of time they may expect infirmities and sickness, old age and death, or death without old age, if Jesus tarries. The doctrine of healing is not like the doctrine of salvation. There many good people have gone far wrong. Yet we must see clearly that God Himself connects the two doctrines inseparably, and God must answer prayer for healing and for other things, as long as He forgives sins. The promise about answered prayer is as definitely for this age as is the promise of forgiveness of confessed sins.

Oh, my brother, believe God and expect Him to answer prayer!

The Bible Never Hints That God Had Changed His Plans of Answering Prayer or That Miracles Have Ceased

Men sometimes say that "the age of miracles is past." But the Bible nowhere hints that there is any change in God's dealings with men in answer to prayer. Men give the plausible argument that miracles were only given to authenticate new covenants and new eras in God's dealing with men. But the trouble with that argument is that it is based on human wisdom and not sustained by a single verse in the Bible.

Elijah did not begin any new period or era in God's dealings with men, yet God worked marvelous miracles in answer to his prayer. Elisha, following him, did not bring any new gospel, yet he worked more miracles than his master. And the Holy Spirit selects Elijah, an Old Testament miracle-working prophet, as a model for New Testament Christians in the matter of prayer. New Testament Christians ought to pray like Elijah and ought to get answers like Elijah, says the Scripture.

If the age of miracles had passed, God would have plainly said so. When the ceremonial law was no longer binding, the Bible said so. In Galatians and Romans we are told that the Jewish ceremonial diet is not binding on New Testament Christians, and that "every creature of God is good" for food. When God changed His plan, He made it known to the people. Likewise, when Jesus, the Lamb of God, came, then animal sacrifices were no longer in order, and Hebrews 10:26 tells us "there remaineth no more sacrifice for sins." The Old Testament had commanded worship at Jerusalem, and sacrifices always in one place (Lev. 17:3-5). But Jesus plainly told the woman of Samaria that "the hour cometh, and now is, when the true worshippers shall worship the Father in spirit and in truth" (John 4:23).

We see clearly this plan, then, that when God changed His way of dealing with people, He plainly told them so. But God has never hinted within the covers of His Holy Bible that He has at any time changed His plan of answering prayer, even to the extent of working miracles. When Jesus said that "all things are possible to him that believeth" in Mark 9:23, and "nothing shall be impossible unto you" in Matthew 17:20, He did not indicate that those were limited promises and good only for the apostolic age. It is wicked and presumptuous for any man to limit the promise which the Lord Jesus Himself gave as unconditional. If the Saviour Himself can be taken at face value and His Word believed, then it is still true, "If ye have faith as a grain of mustard seed, ye shall say unto this mountain, Remove hence to yonder place; and it shall remove; and nothing shall be impossible unto you" (Matt. 17:20). A literal mountain was clearly meant, and elsewhere Jesus said the same thing about a literal sycamine tree (Luke 17:6). If I take the Word of God, then I must believe that Mark 11:24 is good for today. There we are promised, "What things soever ye desire, when ye pray, believe that ye receive them, and ye shall have them." That is the unlimited promise of an unlimited God who answers prayer!

God Wants Us to Pray Big Prayers

Elijah pleased God, not by long prayers but by big prayers! When he prayed for a drouth, he got one three-and-a-half years long, and there was not even dew during that time! (I Kings 17:1). God wants us, like Elijah, to ask big prayers. He reminds us, "Open thy mouth wide and I will fill it." He says, "Is there anything too hard for me?" The prayers of Elijah brought food in famine, brought drouth in judgment, and rain, when Elijah said the word. We Christians today ought to be able to get jobs and food in depression, ought to have rain or drouth, when we ask for it. Food, health, revivals, wonderful works of God, ought to be ours day by day as we call on the Lord God of Elijah. "Where is the Lord God of Elijah?"

"Elias was a man subject to like passions as we are, and

*he prayed earnestly that it might not rain: and it rained not
on the earth by the space of three years and six months.
And he prayed again, and the heaven gave rain, and the
earth brought forth her fruit.”*

Elijah got things because he asked for them. But God
tells us that “ye have not, because ye ask not” (James 4:2).
There are sometimes hindrances to our prayers so that our
prayers are not answered, but far more often we simply
have not because we ask not! The greatest promise in the
New Testament on prayer, I believe, is Matthew 7:7, 8:
“Ask, and it shall be given you; seek, and ye shall find;
knock, and it shall be opened unto you: For every one that
asketh receiveth; and he that seeketh findeth; and to him
that knocketh it shall be opened.” Here we are urged to
ask, seek and knock, and there is the simple unconditional
promise that “every one that asketh receiveth; and he that
seeketh findeth; and to him that knocketh it shall be
opened.” Brother, believe it, do not explain it away. It is
the Word of God and it is for us.

Moody, the unschooled, unordained shoe salesman,
“Crazy Moody,” heard a man say, “The world has yet to
see what God can do with one man absolutely surrendered
to the will of God!” He said, “I will be that man!” Moody
became the evangelist of a phenomenal power who won a
million souls and blessed millions more!

The Saviour told His disciples, “ask, and ye shall
receive, that your joy may be full” (John 16:24).
Doubtless, God would raise up many another Wesley,
Spurgeon, Finney, Moody, Chapman, Torrey, or Sunday
would men but seek and expect and demand and weep for
and claim the same holy power that God freely gave them.

Then let us pray, for “the effectual fervent prayer of a
righteous man availeth much.”

The Lord God of Elijah still lives to answer prayer.

III. WHY FAST AND PRAY?

Christians should sometimes leave off food, sleep, family life or other comforts to pray and do nothing but pray.

The greatest saints of God throughout the Bible often fasted. Fasting is often connected with wholehearted prayer, with mourning, with repentance, with seeking deliverance from enemies or wisdom from above. Moses fasted forty days on Mount Sinai, and our Saviour fasted forty days in the wilderness. The Bible tells how Joshua, David, Ezra, Nehemiah, Daniel, the disciples of John the Baptist, Anna, the apostles, Paul and Barnabas, and others fasted and prayed. Saints of God got their prayers answered when they waited on God with fastings and prayer. Since Bible times, the greatest men of prayer have oftentimes fasted as well as prayed. A Christian is in good company when he fasts and prays.

During the earthly ministry of Christ, the disciples of John the Baptist fasted, the Pharisees fasted, and naturally inquiries were made concerning the disciples of our Saviour. Jesus answered,

"Can ye make the children of the bridechamber fast, while the bridegroom is with them? But the days will come, when the bridegroom shall be taken away from them, and then shall they fast in those days. " —Luke 5:34, 35.

So the Saviour not only fasted, but He also taught His disciples to fast, and they did fast after He was taken away.

The only restriction that our Saviour put upon fasting was that it was to be sincere. Men should not disfigure their faces to appear unto men to fast. A boastful, self-righteous flaunting of religious ceremonies such as that practiced by the Pharisees, hypocrites in the days of our

Lord, is offensive to God, to be sure. But hypocrisy in anything else is a sin as truly as in the case of fasting. Christians should not fast as hypocrites, but they certainly should fast like Jesus fasted, like Paul fasted, like Barnabas and many others fasted.

What Is Fasting and Prayer?

Fasting is such a lost art, so little practiced, so little taught, that we need to consider here what the meaning of fasting is. How does fasting add to prayer? Does it mean simply to abstain from food? Is there virtue in fasting when we do not pray? What is the spiritual significance of fasting?

First, fasting means putting God first. There are times when one ought to eat and praise God for the food. David did when he said, "Bless the Lord, O my soul, and forget not all his benefits. . . Who satisfieth thy mouth with good things; so that thy youth is renewed like the eagle's" (Ps. 103:2, 5). Sometimes eating is the will of God. There are times also when it pleases God for His child to quietly and trustfully lie down to sleep, laying aside all his burdens and sweetly resting in the arms of God's care. "He giveth his beloved sleep" (Ps. 127:2). David could say, "I laid me down and slept; I waked; for the Lord sustained me" (Ps. 3:5).

There are times when men should enjoy the pleasures of family life. "Marriage is honourable in all, and the bed undefiled" (Heb. 13:4). We are told, "Whoso findeth a wife findeth a good thing, and obtaineth favour of the Lord" (Prov. 18:22). "Every good gift and every perfect gift is from above, and cometh down from the Father of lights, with whom is no variableness, neither shadow of turning" (James 1:17). Let us enjoy the blessings of God,

whether food or drink or rest or Christian fellowship, or
home life, or service. Let us give God the glory for them all.
But certainly there are times when we should turn our back
upon everything else in the world but seeking the face of
God. Such times should be times of fasting and prayer.

Fasting, then, should mean that one determines to see
the face of God and for a time, at least, to abstain from
other things in order to give the whole heart to prayer and
waiting on God. Fasting with prayer means to leave off the
lesser blessings for the greater one, the lesser duty for the
far more important duty.

There are times when preachers should quit preaching,
teachers should quit teaching, and all of us should leave off
Bible study even, should even cease to do soul winning, in
order to pray. The apostles said, "We will give ourselves
continually to prayer, and to the ministry of the word"
(Acts 6:4). They put praying before preaching. That is
what Jesus meant when He commanded the disciples not to
depart from Jerusalem but to tarry in Jerusalem as they
prayed for the power of the Holy Spirit before Pentecost.

Thus fasting and prayer simply mean to put prayer first,
before the desire for food, or before anything else that
would take our energy or our attention too much from
prayer.

Ordinarily, fasting means to abstain from food. But the
same spirit will oftentimes lead to abstaining from other
things. Sometimes those who fasted in Bible times fasted by
not taking any kind of drink as well as doing without food.
The men of Nineveh did "not feed, nor drink water"
(Jonah 3:7). Queen Esther and her maidens and Mordecai
and other Jews, before the days of Purim, when Jews were
to be destroyed by the plot of wicked Haman, did not eat
food nor drink water for three days (Esther 4:16). So when
God planned to give the law to Israel from Mount Sinai

the command was given to the people to wash their clothes and "come not at your wives" (Exod. 19:14, 15). And husbands and wives are commanded, "Defraud ye not one the other, except it be with consent for a time, *that ye may give yourselves to fasting and prayer*" (I Cor. 7:5).

The spirit of fasting means that one, for the time being, is willing to abstain from normal and proper duties or pleasures, so he may give himself wholly to the business of prayer. So fasting is really putting God first when you pray, wanting God more than wanting food, more than wanting sleep, more than one wanting fellowship with others, more than wanting to attend to business. How could a Christian ever know that God was first in his life if he did not sometimes turn aside from every other duty and pleasure to give himself wholly to seeking the face of God?

There are many other occasions in life when men do without food. At a football training table, men gladly deprive themselves of sweets and certain foods which are likely to hinder mental alertness and physical fitness and endurance. Should we do less for Jesus Christ? One can run a better race if he has not eaten beforehand. Swimmers know that it is dangerous to eat before swimming lest they suffer from cramps. It is customary for public speakers and singers not to eat until after the important period of concentration and perfect control necessary for their public appearance.

If I can preach better without eating, then why can't I pray better without eating? If a businessman can concentrate better on his figures in some emergency without having his stomach loaded with food, then why cannot a Christian pray better when all his energies are given to that one thing? When people are wholly absorbed in grief for a loved one, they are not hungry and they do not want to eat. Then when one is wholly absorbed in passionate and most earnest prayer, why should he not be glad to do without food?

In truth, when Christians fast it is often true that they have no desire for food. Many, many times I have been so busy about the Lord's work, so absorbed in it that I had no taste for food. Fasting means putting God first in a very intense way, for a period of time and for very definite purposes.

Second, fasting means *persistence* in prayer. We may pray *often,* but most of us do not pray *much.* Our prayers are transitory, indefinite and brief. On the other hand, to fast and pray means that one settles down to the business of praying with a persistence that will take no denial. The widow who haunted the unjust judge with her persistent pleading that he avenge her of her adversary probably neglected her housework while she did it and possibly did not eat (Luke 18:3)! I suppose even the unjust judge did not enjoy his food or his rest, so steadily did she pursue him with her urges!

Real persistence in prayer, letting other things go by and giving God the right of way, often involves fasting. In fact, I think there is little point to fasting or depriving ourselves of other things simply as a matter of self-punishment, if we do not pray. If a man is to be just as absorbed in business as ever, with no more thought for God, then what good would it do him spiritually to do without food, or drink, or sleep? Fasting is the accompaniment of persistent, fervent prayer that will not be denied!

Third, fasting is the deliberate clearing of the way for prayer, laying aside weights and hindrances. In Hebrews 12:1,2 we are commanded: "Wherefore seeing we also are compassed about with so great a cloud of witnesses, let us lay aside every weight, and the sin which doth so easily beset us, and let us run with patience the race that is set before us, Looking unto Jesus the author and finisher of our faith."

Since it is faith that the Holy Spirit is speaking about, and since all the holy examples and witnesses given were by men of persistent, faithful prayer, we surely will make no mistake to interpret this verse as a command to lay aside hindrances to prayer.

"Lay aside every weight." Eating may be good in its place, but certainly sometimes it is a weight that holds down our prayers. Sleep may sometimes be proper, but doubtless many, many times Christians sleep when they ought to be praying. Business in itself may be proper and sometimes men ought to do with their might what their hands find to do, but business, "the cares of this world and the deceitfulness of riches, choke the word, and he becometh unfruitful" (Matt. 13:22).

Fasting is simply laying aside every weight, every hindrance to prayer. A Christian ought, as often as necessary, to be willing to abstain from anything that hinders getting the answer to his prayers; ought to be willing to wait on God until everything that hides the face of God is removed, waiting before God until really he gets the full assurance that his prayer is heard and will be answered to the glory of Christ! When we fast and pray, we are trying to sincerely lay aside anything that hinders our prayers.

Fourth, to fast when we pray ought to be claiming the answer to our prayers. To fast when we pray should mean, "I have set myself to seek God as long as necessary and as earnestly as necessary until He hears me and answers me." It requires faith to pray, for "he that cometh to God must believe that he is, and that he is a rewarder of them that diligently seek him" (Heb. 11:6).

Then it requires *more faith* to fast when we pray.

Fasting pictures greater desire, greater determination, greater faith. One who fasts thereby signifies his sincerity and his confidence that God can be reached, and that God will answer and bless his sincerity and definiteness and willingness to know and do the will of God. Prayer is too often a shallow thing, a light and insincere thing, with Christians. That is surely one reason why so many, many prayers are never answered. Fasting, then, should be simply an evidence of our earnestness, our fervor, our faith.

Fifth, fasting is very properly an expression of mourning. When people are overwhelmed with sorrow, they often do not eat. They have no desire for food. They could not enjoy it. Sometimes when people are overwhelmed with grief, the body will not digest food. Nature itself teaches that fasting is the proper accompaniment and expression of mourning.

In the Bible we have many examples of fasting as an expression of grief. David fasted while he wept over the first child of Bathsheba, when the babe was smitten by the Lord ((II Sam. 12:16, 21). The same spirit must have animated Samuel when he "cried unto the Lord all night" in grief over the rejection of Saul (I Sam. 15:11). That was the spirit of fasting, though the word is not used in that passage. The men of Nineveh fasted, with sackcloth and ashes, a symbol of the deepest mourning (Jonah 3:5-7). As people feast at weddings and other occasions of rejoicing, so they fast at occasions of mourning. Thus the Saviour said that when the Bridegroom was taken away His disciples should fast.

Hence, those who are in sorrow do well sometimes to fast as they seek the comfort of God's face. Those who have sinned and grieve in penitence do well to fast as they turn their hearts from sin and confess their failures and faults and try to make restitution. Fasting fits exactly with repentance and with sorrow for sin.

Things We Can Get by Fasting and Prayer

Fasting is an aid and adjunct of prayer. Some things never come to a child of God "but by prayer and fasting." If prayer is good, then more prayer is better. If earnest prayer pleases God, then sometimes, surely, He is pleased when the prayer is so earnest that we do not want food nor drink nor sleep nor any other ordinary pleasure. If God is pleased for us to seek Him, then sometimes, surely, it pleases Him for us to lay aside every weight, abstain from everything that might absorb our energy and interest and thought, that we may give ourselves wholly to the matter of prayer.

We name here some things that Christians have a right to seek by prayer and fasting; things which God has, in times past, given His people because of their prayer with fasting.

1. Help in time of trouble often comes from fasting and prayer.

God says, "Call upon me in the day of trouble; I will deliver thee, and thou shalt glorify me" (Ps. 50:15). A time of trouble is a good time to pray. If it is a good time to pray, and if the trouble is severe, then it is a good time to fast, too. Joshua and the elders of Israel remained prostrate before the ark of God from morning until evening without eating, after the Israelites were defeated by the men of Ai (Josh. 7:6). It was a time of great distress, of defeat, of shame and of fear. The very destiny of the nation seemed at stake. When they fasted and prayed, God showed them the sin that hindered victory.

When in the days of the Judges the eleven tribes of Israel came up against Benjamin by God's command, and when 40,000 were slain in two days, "Then all the children of Israel, and all the people, went up, and came unto the house of God, and wept, and sat there before the Lord, and fasted that day until the even" (Judges 20:26). In their defeat and sorrow they wept and fasted and called on God. God heard and delivered them and the next day gave victory. Defeat is a fine time to pray and fast!

When Queen Esther and Mordecai and the Jews in captivity were in danger of being blotted out as a race, they fasted and prayed. Their trouble led to sincere and fervent prayer, such praying that they did not eat nor drink. When Ezra feared the brigands of the wilderness, he called a fast at the river Ahava (Ezra 8:21-23). The time of trouble is a proper time for fasting and prayer.

Let all those who are in trouble call upon God. If you find difficulty in getting an answer from Heaven, then fast and pray, sincerely laying everything else aside, as far as necessary, to seek God's face and find His will and blessing.

2. To find what is wrong, what displeases God, we should sometimes fast and pray.

When Joshua and the elders of Israel did not know why God had allowed them to be defeated at Ai, they fasted and prayed until God showed them the sin of Achan and about the hidden wedge of gold, the silver and the Babylonish garment. Many a Christian who does not prosper could learn the reason if they would wait before God in such sincerity and abandonment of self that they would not eat, would not sleep, would not carry on the regular affairs of life until God revealed what was wrong. We once set a day of fasting and prayer Sunday at the Fundamentalist Baptist Church in Dallas that we might know, as far as possible, the full meaning that God had for us in the burning of our church. We wanted God to lay bare our hearts and show us the things in which He was displeased.

3. Genuine repentance sometimes involves fasting and prayer.

One may confess his sins without repenting of them. Unless we deliberately take time for meditation and examination of our hearts and waiting on God, often we have no real sense of sin, no genuine horror at our guilt. I know that in order to be saved one may turn to Christ as soon as he knows himself a sinner and knows that Christ died for him, if he will. But alas, many times those of us who are already saved have trouble turning our hearts away from sin!

I believe in Bible times God's saints often took time to fast and wait before God in order that they might genuinely, with contrite heart, forsake their sins and mourn over them. In Zechariah 12:10-14 we are told how, at the second coming of Christ, the Jews will mourn over Christ "as one mourneth for his only son, and shall be in bitterness for him, as one that is in bitterness for his firstborn." And that mourning in Jerusalem over their sins will be as great as the mourning in the Valley of Megiddo over the dead! Every family shall mourn apart, and their wives apart. This evidently pictures the broken hearts of people who long to turn away from their sins and who take time to see the enormity of their sin in rejecting the Saviour.

We are commanded, "Be afflicted, and mourn, and weep: let your laughter be turned to mourning, and your joy to heaviness. Humble yourselves in the sight of the

Lord, and he shall lift you up" (James 4:9,10).

I know God is merciful and ready to instantly forgive all who sincerely turn in the heart to Him. But I too know that oftentimes our pretended turning to God is insincere and shallow, with no real sorrow for sin, no effort at restitution, and no genuine change in attitude of heart. The ghastly wickedness of sin is hidden from us lighthearted moderns. Surely it would often please God if we took time apart to search our hearts and find what displeases God and wholly forsake, as far as we can consciously do so, our sins. If we spend enough time in prayer we can learn the meaning of the old song,

> **Come Holy Spirit, Heavenly dove,**
> **Sweet messenger of rest**
> **I hate the sins that made Thee mourn,**
> **And drove Thee from my breast.**

Fasting will help us break up the fallow ground of our hearts.

4. Fasting and prayer often lead to victory over sin.

The world has many Christians who have trusted Christ, who sincerely love Him, who are going to Heaven—yet Christians who have no daily victory over sin. Everywhere I go I find Christians who say they cannot quit cigarettes, cannot control their tempers, have trouble in surrendering even enough to give God regularly the tithe. Christians find it hard to forgive one another and are constantly falling under the temptation of Satan.

Is there victory for such Christians? Yes there is, but sometimes it is found only in the time of fasting and prayer, waiting on God and laying aside every weight, every duty, every pleasure that might interfere with our wholehearted prayers.

Many times I have seen things happen in protracted seasons of prayer that would not happen in the ordinary course of events. In an all-night prayer meeting a number of men, including a young preacher, gave up tobacco. One Christian man confessed to his pastor his sin of enmity and gossip. A grown son, now on the foreign mission field, confessed his violent temper and mistreatment of his mother, and gained courage to right the wrong he had done.

In days of fasting and prayer, when God is put first, when the heart has been searched, when sins have been confessed, when restitution has been made, when one's will is surrendered to God, then God has often done great things for the penitent beggar who waits before Him. We need not think that our hunger gains any favor with God. No, God has abundant mercy for all our needs, and we cannot, need not, buy it. But on the other hand, God does want sincerity and fervor and single-heartedness in our praying. Every Christian, I think, should occasionally fast and pray, wait before God until he gets the victory that he needs.

I remember with great joy how one night I waited before God alone in my room until 1:30 begging Him for victory over some things in my own life, and begging also for the power of the Spirit on the revival in which I was engaged. God gloriously heard and answered in both matters.

If you do not have victory over sin, then wait before God and pay whatever price is necessary to secure His favor and the assurance of His help.

5. *Heavenly wisdom received in prayer and fasting.*

In Acts 13:1-3 we have a remarkable incident showing how men who fasted and prayed got direct leadership of the Holy Spirit. Here is that sweet passage:

"Now there were in the church that was at Antioch certain prophets and teachers; as Barnabas, and Simeon that was called Niger, and Lucius of Cyrene, and Manaen, which had been brought up with Herod the tetrarch, and Saul. As they ministered to the Lord, and fasted, the Holy Ghost said, Separate me Barnabas and Saul for the work whereunto I have called them. And when they had fasted and prayed, and laid their hands on them, they sent them away."

Notice that "as they ministered to the Lord, and fasted," the Holy Ghost told them who to send, that is, Barnabas and Saul. Notice again that "when they had fasted and prayed, and laid their hands on them, they sent them away." Twice in that short passage we are told that these prophets and teachers fasted. They fasted as they prayed for wisdom. They fasted as they prayed for power upon these men whom they were sending forth as the first foreign missionaries in New Testament times. And when these men laid their hands upon the heads of Paul and Barnabas and sent them away, they were "sent forth by the Holy Ghost." And marvelous wonders attended their ministry!

We, too, could have plain leading, we could know the will of God, we could have a plain path for our feet, if we were but willing to wait before the Lord, ministering unto Him, fasting and praying! You have a problem about raising your family, about making a living, about where you should serve Christ, about what course you should take in some particular matter—does not God hear your prayer for wisdom? Do you have doubts and troubles and no assurance or peace of mind? Then why not just set a time and wait before God until you get the answer? If it takes fasting as well as praying, if it takes giving up other matters, then do it and get the blessing that God has for you. You can find the will of God if you seek it sincerely, unstintedly and without limit, in fasting and prayer.

6. *Intercession for others is answered when we fast and pray.*

Most of our praying is for ourselves. Yet every Christian surely admits his responsibility to pray for others. Do you pray for your pastor? for some foreign missionary? Do you pray regularly for some unsaved loved one? Do you pray for someone who has asked you to help bear the burden of his load day by day, whatever it is? Well, our own needs take up most of the time in our little, puny, short praying. If you would pray for others, pray happily, pray with assurance that you are heard, then take time to pray through. And any long, extended time of fervent prayer, may also involve fasting. It takes more than a little short prayer to rid us of our own selfishness. We have, each one of us, so many needs that we will not do our duty in praying for others unless we take an extended time for it, unless we really wait long before God in order to get out of our selfishness and get victory over our own immediate needs.

Would you be an intercessor? Do you want to learn to pray for others? Then set aside long periods in which to pray, with sufficient time to search your heart and to know the mind of Christ. Take time without the distraction of eating and drinking or sleeping perhaps, and God will surely give you part of the blessed burden that is on Jesus Christ, the burden that is for others.

7. *Holy Spirit power comes in answer to fasting and prayer.*

There are many things for which we can pray and at once receive the answer. I believe that a sinner can trust in

Christ and be saved at once, without delay. The thief on the cross had only to ask, and he was forgiven. The Publican in the Temple had only to say, "God be merciful to me a sinner" and he went down to his house justified. I know of no Scripture that teaches that a lost sinner needs to beg and plead and so try to touch the heart of God or afflict himself in order to be saved. When the poor sinful will is ready to surrender and put his trust in Christ, then God is immediately ready to forgive and save.

However, though God is instantly willing to forgive the sinner, there are other matters about which we should expect to pray longer. Certainly one of the blessed teachings of the Saviour, emphasized many times, is that we should be persistent in prayer. The widow before the unjust judge prayed again and again (Luke 18:1-8). Teaching the disciples to pray, Jesus first gave them the model prayer called the Lord's Prayer, and then told them about the neighbor who came and pounded on the door at midnight saying, "A friend of mine in his journey is come to me and I have nothing to set before him. Lend me three loaves" (Luke 11:1-13). In that case certainly the man asking for bread was asking for it for another who had none. And Jesus told exactly what He meant in that parable when He said in verse 13, "If ye then, being evil, know how to give good gifts unto your children: how much more shall your heavenly Father give the Holy Spirit to them that ask him?" Notice the Holy Spirit was given to them "that ASK him." Ask how? Ask like that neighbor who knocked on the door again and again and even then only received "because of his importunity." That illustrates a Christian begging God for bread to take to sinners, or, in others words, praying for the power of the Holy Spirit to make him a soul winner! And I understand the word "ask" in Greek is in the imperfect or continuing tense, and it means to them that keep on asking God will give the Holy Spirit.

Certainly before Pentecost the disciples "continued steadfastly in prayer and supplication" (Acts 1:14). And otherwise, I feel sure they would not have received the blessings that God gave them. They prayed, but they more than prayed—they *begged* God. That isn't all. They doubtless fasted as well. Jesus had said about His disciples, "But the days will come, when the bridegroom shall be taken away from them, and then shall they fast in those days" (Luke 5:35).

Jesus had just been taken away, and now the disciples, children of the bride-chamber, fasted as they prayed and begged God for the power to get about His business! They prayed, yes, but they fasted as they prayed. I do not know that it specially matters that they just did without food. What matters is that they turned their hearts wholly, unreservedly, and without interruption, to the business of getting all the power God had for them, and being possessed and covered and filled with the Holy Spirit Himself!

When Peter came to preach the Gospel to Cornelius and his household, Cornelius said to him, "Four days ago I was fasting until this hour; and at the ninth hour I prayed in my house. . ." (Acts 10:30). Perhaps that is part of the secret as to why Cornelius and his household were filled with the Holy Spirit at the same time they were saved. This is the only specific instance on record in the Bible, as far as I know, where people were filled with the Holy Spirit at the same time they were saved. Evidently all the heart-searching, all the surrendering of the will, all the confession of sin, all the yielding of the heart that was necessary for Cornelius to be filled with the Holy Spirit, was already done by the time he learned how to be saved!

When Paul was converted he fasted and prayed three days and nights before he was filled with the Holy Spirit. Read carefully the ninth chapter of Acts and you will see that Paul was converted as described in verses 4 and 5. Verse 9 tells that he went three days without sight, "and neither did eat nor drink." The angel told Ananias, "behold, he prayeth," in verse 11. Those three days of fasting and prayer fitted Paul to be filled with the Holy Spirit, and in verse 17 we learn that Ananias went to him, sent by the Lord, "that thou mightest receive thy sight, *and be filled with the Holy Ghost.*" Certainly fasting and prayer are appropriate for Christians who want to be filled with the Holy Spirit.

Let us turn again to the sending forth of Barnabas and Paul in Acts 13:1-4. These prophets and teachers fasted until they knew the will of God. Then they fasted and prayed further until they could lay their hands upon Paul and Barnabas in power and they could go away "being sent forth by the Holy Ghost."

It was the experience of D. L. Moody, of R. A. Torrey, of Charles G. Finney, as it has been of many other Christians greatly used in soul winning, that they were filled with the Holy Spirit after a long season of waiting before God, surrendering self, being molded on God's potter's wheel.

Dear Christian, if you want help in trouble, then pray, and if the answer does not come easily and soon, fast and pray. Fasting and prayer, by which we mean wholehearted, surrendered, fervent, determined praying, will help you to find what is wrong. Fasting and prayer will help you to genuinely repent and turn from sin, will help you to get victory over bad habits, grudges, daily temptation, will help you to find the wisdom of God and leadership of the Holy Spirit, will help you to intercede for others, and will open the way for you to receive the power of the Holy Spirit in abundance.

Dear child of God, do you feel led to try it? Then fast and pray till God meets you in blessing.

3.

PROSPERITY AND SUCCESS FROM GOD'S WELL OF JOY

"Whatsoever he doeth shall prosper."—Ps. 1:3.

"That thou mayest prosper whithersoever thou goest."—Josh. 1:7.

"For then thou shalt make thy way prosperous, and then thou shalt have good success."—Josh. 1:8.

Many people do not take the Bible seriously. They think it has little to do with the practical affairs of life. A great many Christians, and even preachers, foolishly say that the Bible and Bible religion are good enough for spiritual things but they cannot give any guarantee of prosperity in this life. It is taken for granted that being a Christian and living by the Bible cannot help a man make a living for his family, to have a job in hard times, and to prosper financially and materially.

But such an idea is contrary to the Bible. The Bible does give a clear rule for prosperity and success in every detail of a man's life, including both spiritual happiness and material comfort.

Certainly we will grant that God does not want everybody to be rich. He does not even want people to desire riches. We are told that "the love of money is the root of all evil" (I Tim. 6:10), and covetousness is mentioned as one of the ten great sins prohibited by the

Ten Commandments. God does not usually want His children to be millionaires.

But on the other hand, God does not want them to be defeated and in want. I am certain that God is displeased and dishonored by the multitude of church members who are on relief, professing Christians who fail in all they put their hand to, people who are the pity and the burden of all who successfully and prosperously meet life's obligations.

A glance at several verses will show that God wants His people to have all good things, including sufficient food and raiment and other necessities of life.

"No good thing will he withhold from them that walk uprightly."—Ps. 84:11.

"But seek ye first the kingdom of God, and his righteousness; and all these things shall be added unto you."—Matt. 6:33.

"Honour the Lord with thy substance, and with the firstfruits of all thine increase: So shall thy barns be filled with plenty, and thy presses shall burst out with new wine."—Prov. 3:9, 10.

"But my God shall supply all your needs according to his riches in glory by Christ Jesus."—Phil. 4:19.

In Psalm 37 are a number of promises of material blessings. For instance, verse 3 says, "Trust in the Lord, and do good; so shalt thou dwell in the land, and verily thou shalt be fed." The same Psalm clearly shows that God wants His people to earn their way. He does not want them to come to begging and they need not do so, for verse 25 says, "I have been young and now am old; yet have I not seen the righteous forsaken, nor his seed begging bread."

How Have This Prosperity?

If God wants His people to be prosperous, there should

be very definite instructions about it in the Bible. And there are. Many verses tell how to have the blessing of God on daily life.

Psalm 1, verses 1-3, gives a clear and useful rule for prosperity:

"Blessed is the man that walketh not in the counsel of the ungodly, nor standeth in the way of sinners, nor sitteth in the seat of the scornful. But his delight is in the law of the Lord; and in his law doth he meditate day and night. And he shall be like a tree planted by the rivers of water, that bringeth forth his fruit in his season; his leaf also shall not wither; and whatsoever he doeth shall prosper."

The word "blessed" means fortunate, happy, or prosperous. The happy man mentioned here does not keep bad company. Notice the three verbs, "walketh," "standeth," and "sitteth." The man who first casually walks with bad company will next stand in the way with them and then sit down in their seat and live with them.

Notice again how the kind of company grows worse. First, "ungodly"—those not Christians. Second, "sinners"—those actively sinning and wicked; and third, the "scorners"—those who are unbelievers, who scoff at and hate God.

This blessed man or happy man is the one who keeps out of bad company. This is one thing important about God's plan for our prosperity and success.

Root of Prosperity, the Bible

But the Bible itself is the secret of prosperity and success. "The fear of the Lord is the beginning of wisdom" (Prov. 9:10). True wisdom or knowledge of how to succeed and do well should naturally come from the Bible, the Word of

God. All success depends upon the favor of God, and we cannot know how to please God except from the Bible.

So verse 2 says,

"But his delight is in the law of the Lord; and in his law doth he meditate day and night."

The happy, successful, and prosperous man is the man who loves the Bible, reads the Bible, lives by the Bible, and meditates therein day and night!

At once it becomes apparent that some men are not prosperous who seem to be. I believe God can help in financial affairs and give prosperity in business, but I am certain that those who only prosper in material matters are miserable failures. God can help people make money, but money is of far less importance than spiritual welfare and happiness. True prosperity is based on one's harmony with the will of God, and one cannot be in harmony with the will of God without a delight in the Word of God and constant meditation therein. Any other prosperity is one-sided, incomplete, and often temporary, more apparent than real. Real prosperity, well-rounded, complete, permanent prosperity and good fortune is found by loving, learning, following, and meditating in the Word of God.

To be fully prosperous a man must be blessed, not only when he deals in money but when he deals in eternal values; not only in bread and meat but in love, joy, peace, longsuffering, gentleness, goodness, faith, meekness, temperance, etc. This prosperity is described in the third verse of Psalm 1 as follows:

"And he shall be like a tree planted by the rivers of water, that bringeth forth his fruit in his season; his leaf also shall not wither; and whatsoever he doeth shall prosper."

A cut flower may bloom and live for a time in a vase of water. The dry land of a great desert not long ago was watered by an unusual rain, the first in years. Immediately there sprang up lovely wild flowers from the seeds long dormant. But as the moisture evaporated, the flowers died.

So is the occasional and partial prosperity of any man whose roots take hold on the things of this world. But the happy, fortunate, blessed man of the first Psalm who meditates day and night in the Word of God and delights in it is like the tree planted by the riverside and those roots go down deep to the subsoil, eternally washed by the abundant river! Such a Christian never dries up.

Throughout western Texas and much other country of little rainfall, the observer may see the prairie broken by trees only along the water courses. Creeks are marked by the trees which grow along their banks. Trees cannot grow in the dry soil on higher ground, in wide stretches of the western United States.

The depression has ruined many businesses because they did not have resources to draw on at a time of distress. When moral stresses come, many men and women fail and fall before the temptation and troubles that are theirs. The breakdown of business institutions and bankruptcy of firms is not as bad as the failing of human character in time of stress. Many people cannot stand prosperity and cannot stand poverty. They wither and are miserable, unhappy failures in the face of the inevitable disaster that life brings. Their roots are not planted deep by the rivers of water. They do not have a place to go for reserve strength for every need. But the man who delights in the Bible and meditates therein day and night is like the tree planted by the river of water. Such a man will bring forth his fruit in his season whether it be a dry season or a wet season. His prosperity will not depend upon outward conditions but will depend on him being in touch with God, having prayers answered and having the smile of Heaven upon his efforts.

The Fruitful Christian

The fruitful Christian is one with his roots in the Word of God, one who delights in the Bible and meditates therein day and night. A Christian who is not successful in soul winning is a Christian who is not doing right by the Bible. Soul winning does not depend upon education, upon training, upon natural gifts. No tree can bring forth fruit of itself. It must be able to reach down deep in the bosom of mother nature and draw up the life-giving water and the food which is in the soil. So Christians only bear fruit as they are rooted deep by the rivers of water of God's Word.

Soul winners are not always great Bible students, not always scholars. But successful and unusual soul winners are always those who delight in the Word of God, who believe it, who love it, who meditate upon it.

D. L. Moody is a suitable example. He was not known as a great Bible student. He was not a scholar. He had a very limited education. Yet he was a great Bible preacher and soul winner. He loved the Bible with a holy devotion, studied it, knew it, believed it, and meditated in it day and night. Others who have scholarship do not delight and meditate day and night in the Word of God and so they do not bring forth fruit in season as they could and should.

The Christian Whose Leaf Does Not Wither

The leaves of a tree have many useful functions. As the roots absorb the moisture and food values from the soil, so the leaves use the sunshine to carry on the process of nature. The leaves are a shade to the birds in the tree and to man and beasts who rest beneath its shelter. The leaves delight the eye. Anyone who will study carefully the infinite variety in the shapes and color of the leaves will realize at once that God intended them for beauty.

The Christian whose roots are deep in God's Word, Christians like a tree planted by the rivers of water, will have leaves that do not wither! Surely this means a happy, happy Christian life. Christians ought to win souls, but Christians ought also to be happy, joyful, sweet-tempered. A Christian's leaves should not wither. And his leaf will not wither if he delights day and night in the Word of God!

One of my sins as a preacher has been that sometimes I labor in the ministry until I lose my own joy in the Lord. Too often I study the Bible as a preacher but do not study it as a Christian. Too often I feed others but have no food for my own poor withered soul! Sometimes I cry out with the one in the Song of Solomon: "They made me the keeper of the vineyards; but mine own vineyard have I not kept" (1:6). I am saying that sometimes I am a Christian with withered leaves.

Of course after your leaves wither your fruit will begin to fail. I have found it so in my own life. The tree that is thrifty and healthful with an abundant crop of leaves should be expected to bear fruit. So Christians ought to be so happy, so content, so easy to get along with, so full of the Christian graces that every passer-by will attest the genuineness of their religion. What a sin for Christians to have withered leaves, drooping faces, discontented hearts!

When I feel the joy slipping, I know I need to go back with a new abandon to the Word of God, to love it, to delight in it, to meditate in it day and night. When I do that I can learn to rejoice again in the Lord, and there is a freshness to my ministry that otherwise would be lacking.

A peach tree that I knew about died and the leaves

withered and began to fall just as the peaches began to ripen. The thrifty housewife gathered the peaches, but they were not good to eat fresh. They made sour pickles very well! Christians would not bear so much sour fruit if their leaves were always green.

George Mueller was a great man of prayer. He said that he had kept a record of ten thousand prayers of his which God had answered. He said that the first duty of every Christian every morning is to become happy in the Lord, before asking for a thing else. He got to where he read and meditated in the Word of God until he estimated that he read ten pages of the Bible to one of all other literature!

One of the first duties of a Christian is to be close enough to God and to be happy in Him. And remember that this greenness of leaf comes by having one's roots deep by the river of waters, the unfailing stream of Divine revelation, the Word of God!

Oh if hungry-hearted, defeated people would only learn the joy and blessing of an intimate knowledge and loving meditation day and night in the Word of God!

"In His Law Doth He Meditate Day and Night"

To fulfill the requirements of this passage, the daylight is not enough. It will take some of the nights. Christians should so delight in the Bible that they will meditate therein in the night as well as in the day. Gamblers have been known to gamble through two or three days and nights without stopping for sleep, so great is the greed for unholy, unearned gain. People often dance all night without sleep. Many a man with an active mind has read other books all night long. Work is more precious than sleep to many, and pleasure is a greater rival still. Why would it be strange for a child of God to sometimes delight in the Word of God all the night through?

This Scripture anticipates that the Word of God will so saturate the blessed man's being that he can meditate on the Word while he works. I well remember how the first talks I ever made for Jesus were prepared as I milked the cows and meditated on the Scriptures. And the Christian who loves the Bible and meditates therein will memorize a great many passages which he can rejoice in at night when the lights are out, or in the day when his hands are too busy to hold THE BOOK.

"Whatsoever He Doeth Shall Prosper"

Again I remind you that the Bible has many wonderful "whosoevers" and "whatsoevers." It has some wonderful "alls" and "nones." The Bible uses sweeping, positive, all-inclusive, all-exclusive language. And praise His name, God always means all He says.

Men sometimes say that things are "great" when they are ordinary. Men say "thousands" when they should say "hundreds." But when God says "whatsoever" He means exactly that. The blessed Christian who delights in the Bible and meditates therein day and night has the unfailing rule of success and prosperity in everything he puts his hand to—"whatsoever he doeth shall prosper!" Preachers who constantly delight in the Word of God and meditate therein will have blessing on every sermon, will have blessing on his personal work, will have wisdom from God for all his decisions. He will have money to pay his rent, his gas and to buy the groceries he needs. And so it will be with every Christian, preacher or not. The saved man may expect everything he turns his hand to to be blessed, if he first has his roots planted deep in the Word of God and if day and night he meditates and delights in the presence and will of Christ as revealed therein. This is God's unfailing rule for prosperity in everything you do.

I promised God I would try to claim this promise. On that basis THE SWORD OF THE LORD and the book ministry have been blessed. On that basis God has given health, help in the office and supplied our financial needs day by day. I have failed to keep my part of the bargain much of the time, and sometimes as a result I did not bear fruit in season and my leaves began to wither. But I have definitely proved to my own soul that the Word of God is true.

Prosperity will come in every detail of the Christian's life—in food, clothes, sweet friendships, health, in inward happiness, in religious activities—if he gives himself with holy abandonment to delight and meditate in the Bible day and night.

Read the Bible Through This Year

Many things a Christian should do with the Bible. He should read it and hear it read (Rev. 1:3). He should 'search the Scriptures' (John 5:39). He should memorize much of it, hiding it in his heart (Ps. 119:11). He should meditate in the Bible continually, and certainly he should heed it and live by its precepts.

We cannot consider other duties toward the Bible in this short chapter, but certainly all should read the Bible. The Bible has less than twelve hundred chapters. If you read four chapters a day, you can read the entire Bible, both Old and New Testaments, in about ten months. Or you can read three chapters on week days and five chapters on Sunday and read all the Bible in less than a year. The average Christian has never read the Bible through, though it would only take about thirty minutes a day even for a slow reader. What a shame! The time spent on the daily newspaper by the average Christian would make him a good Bible student, reading through the entire Word of God every year.

I suggest that every Christian who reads this start out to love the Bible, learn the Bible and meditate in the Bible. In as far as you do what God has said, you will find prosperity in every detail of life.

The Promise Repeated

Many other Scriptures could be quoted, but Joshua 1:7, 8 gives such definite promise for prosperity and success that we quote it here:

"Only be thou strong and very courageous, that thou mayest observe to do according to all the law, which Moses my servant commanded thee: turn not from it to the right hand or to the left, that thou mayest prosper whithersoever thou goest. This book of the law shall not depart out of thy mouth; but thou shalt meditate therein day and night, that thou mayest observe to do according to all that is written therein: for then thou shalt make thy way prosperous, and then thou shalt have good success."

Try God's good plan for prosperity for the next year and it will really be a "happy and prosperous new year," the most truly happy and prosperous that you have ever spent.

4.

GIVING: A SURE WAY OF JOY AND BLESSING

If you do not tithe, I know what is wrong with you. Not being a tither shows a man up if he is a Christian. If you do not tithe, I believe I can show you five unanswerable reasons why you ought to.

By tithing I mean giving God one-tenth of your income. Not one-tenth of your savings, not one-tenth of what you have left after you pay your debts, but one-tenth of your salary, or one-tenth of what your farm produces, or one-tenth of the net income from your business.

Tithing means to turn over a dime out of every dollar to the Lord. And of course it involves giving God the *first* dime. If you do not give God the first dime, you may not give Him a dime at all. The Bible teaches that everything you have and everything you get is the Lord's and that He requires you to give for His work at least a tenth of it to Him and freewill offerings besides, as the Holy Spirit leads. But here are the five reasons for it. Check them by your Bible, face the question honestly and see whether you are an obedient Christian, an honest Christian, a loving Christian, a grateful Christian, a believing Christian.

I. OBEDIENCE

God commanded, "Bring ye all the tithes into the

storehouse" (Mal. 3:10). That is a plain command. You are commanded to bring God all the tithes. Then in the New Testament, to those who paid tithes of everything, even of the mint and of the anise and the cummin, small herbs or spices of their garden, Jesus said, "These ought ye to have done" (Matt. 23:23).

Then again Paul, writing by the Holy Spirit to the church at Corinth, commanded proportionate giving. He said, "Upon the first day of the week let every one of you lay by him in store as God hath prospered him" (I Cor. 16:2). God here commands New Testament Christians to give each week a certain proportion of what God has prospered them with during the week. It is a plain command.

What proportion did He mean? Did He mean one-half? Or one-twentieth? Or one-fifth? Remember that all these Christians had only the Old Testament. Paul preached from the Old Testament because the New was not yet written and collected. And of course, the proportion commanded was the same kind God commanded throughout the Old Testament, and repeatedly mentions also in the New, that, is the tithe, or one-tenth.

So there it is, Christian; it is the plain command of God to tithe. If you do not tithe, you are a disobedient Christian. You do not follow the plain commands of God. There is no use to say that you are trying to serve God or that you are surrendered to His will, or that you will do whatever He says, until you fully surrender to do what He says on the money question.

Somebody says that the tithe is now out of date because it was in the Old Testament. Some even say it was a part of the ceremonial law, though it began long before the law was given. Abraham tithed (Gen. 14:20). Jacob tithed (Gen. 28:22). Both of these grew rich under the blessing of

God by tithing. And this was long before the law was given at Mount Sinai.

But even if it were part of the Mosaic law, it is not ceremonial but moral law to tithe. When God had ceremonies put away, He mentions them particularly. He said, "There remaineth no more sacrifice for sins" (Heb. 10:26). So the ceremony of animal sacrifices is done away. Then again the ceremonial law about diet, forbidding to eat pork and catfish, etc., is plainly done away, and God said, "What God hath cleansed, that call not thou common" (Acts 10:15). And again the Scripture says, "Every creature of God is good, and nothing to be refused, if it be received with thanksgiving: for it is sanctified by the word of God and prayer" (I Tim. 4:4, 5). And so the New Testament plainly said that we were to do away with circumcision (Gal. 5:6; Gal. 6:15). When God did away with ceremonies of the Mosaic law, He said so.

But where is the Scripture that says anything about doing away with tithes? You will not find it in the Bible! God says, "Bring ye all the tithes." He said, "The tithe. . .is the Lord's" (Lev. 27:30). Tithing is the test of an obedient Christian. You are not obeying God if you do not give at least as much as a tithe.

II. HONESTY

The second reason for tithing is that honesty requires it. Those who do not tithe are dishonest and rob God. That is the plain teaching of the Word of God. "Will a man rob God? Yet ye have robbed me. But ye say, Wherein have we robbed thee? In tithes and offerings. Ye are cursed with a curse: for ye have robbed me, even this whole nation" (Mal. 3:8, 9).

There it is. If you do not tithe and do not bring offerings

also, then you have robbed God, and you are dishonest. Honesty requires that one tithe and give offerings.

Again I remind you that honesty is not a part of the ceremonial law but of the moral law. Which one of the Ten Commandments will cover the question of tithing? The eighth, which says, "Thou shalt not steal" (Exod. 20:15). Stealing or robbing is just as big a sin in the New Testament as in the Old Testament, and God says that those who do not bring tithes and offerings to God are robbers. Do not get mad at me but get mad at God if you do not like that.

Will a man rob God? Well, God says that men do, that they rob Him in tithes and offerings and that they therefore are cursed with a curse!

So if you are just bound to be a thief or crooked in money matters, don't you think you had better steal from somebody else besides God? Would it not be better for you to cheat somebody else instead of the God who made you? Remember that He gives you everything you ever have in this world. How wicked to rob God!

Some men think that they do not owe God anything. They never consider it dishonesty to steal from God. That is human and carnal, but Christians ought to have the Bible viewpoint. And the Bible plainly says, "The earth is the Lord's, and the fulness thereof; the world and they that dwell therein" (Ps. 24:1). God says that the cattle on a thousand hills are His (Ps. 50:10). And because all belongs to God, He demands the tithe, and it is rightfully His. He also demands offerings as the Holy Spirit leads. They are rightfully His, according to the teaching of the Bible.

You who do not tithe and do not bring offerings to God, when you get down to pray just remember that God says you have robbed Him, and see how you feel then about praying!

III. LOVE

Real love will lead a Christian to give both tithes and offerings. Nothing in the world will loosen the purse strings and make an old stingy tightwad into a rejoicing free-hearted, liberal man, like a good old-fashioned case of the love of God shed abroad in his heart by the Holy Spirit! You remember that Jesus said, "If ye love me, keep my commandments" (John 14:15), and again He said, "If a man love me, he will keep my words" (John 14:23). There it is as clear as day! If you love God as you ought to, you will do right about tithes and offerings and keep His commandments.

All the threats in the world will not make a child obey his parents as well as real filial love. All the vows of the marriage altar will not make a man take care of his wife as a real case of unselfish love. And so you can just put it down that something is badly wrong with a man's heart if he is not willing to do what God said about tithes and offerings.

Note that love makes it easy to give. I remember how once Mrs. Rice and I were very carefully tithing, even to the pennies, our small income when we first married and went to the seminary to prepare to preach the Gospel. But one day I saw how little and stingy that was, and I said, "This doesn't represent the way I love the Lord. One dime out of every dollar will not begin to show how I love Him for all He has done for me." So from that very day on we began to give far more than a tithe, and what a joy it has been!

And that is one reason why I know that New Testament Christians ought to give as much as Old Testament Christians did. If you love God as Abraham did, of course you will want to give tithes of all and more just as

Abraham did. If you meet God in some lonely place and He comforts your heart and blesses you and supplies all your needs, surely you, like Jacob, will love God enough to give as much as Jacob gave.

Do you really believe that an Old Testament Jew under the law ought to love God any more than a New Testament Christian under grace? Do you really believe that all the quibbles you can raise will excuse your stingy heart when you simply do not love God enough to do as much as Jews were required to do under the law? No, I am certain that real love will bring to God just as much now as when righteous Abel brought of the firstlings of his flock, or when spiritual Jews brought tithes and offerings to the Lord.

When love waxed cold, then the Jews robbed God. So today when a child of God grows stingy and covetous and worldly-minded, he robs God for lack of love.

If you love God, surely you will keep His command about tithes and offerings.

IV. GRATITUDE

The fourth reason for tithing is gratitude. If you are grateful for all the goodness of God, then surely you will show it by answering His goodness. How liberal God has been! Every day He pours upon you blessings too many to name.

> Count your blessings, name them one by one,
> Count your blessings, see what God has done.
> Count your blessings, name them one by one,
> And it will surprise you what the Lord has done.

And here again it is easy to tell whether we ought to give as much as the Jews did under law. Would you rather be a

Jew dwelling in the darkness of Old Testament times, looking into the dim future, and trusting that God would some day send a Saviour, and blindly offering sacrifices? or would you rather be a New Testament Christian with an open Bible, a printed Bible including both the Old and New Testaments, and knowing that Christ has already come and has already paid for man's sins? Who ought to love God better—New Testament Christians or Old Testament Jews? You need not talk to me about the gratitude of your heart for all God's blessings if you do not feel grateful enough to give Him everything that He asks.

V. FAITH

If you do not tithe, it is because you do not believe the plain statements of God's Word. Again and again He has promised that He will repay, that He will prosper you financially, that you will be better off even in material things because of tithes and offerings. If you believed it, you would tithe. When you do not bring the tithes and offerings for the Lord's work, it simply shows that you do not believe He will do what He said.

People say to me, "Brother Rice, I would like to tithe, but I can't afford to. If I tithed, I simply could not pay for the necessities of life. I could not meet my bills." Little do you realize it, but you are simply saying that it does not pay to serve God, that you cannot depend upon His promises, and that really He would not pay you back. You do not believe the Bible!

"Bring ye all the tithes into the storehouse, that there may be meat in mine house, and prove me now herewith, saith the Lord of hosts, if I will not open you the windows of heaven, and pour you out a blessing, that there shall not be room enough to receive it. And I will rebuke the

devourer for your sakes, and he shall not destroy the fruits of your ground; neither shall your vine cast her fruit before the time in the field, saith the Lord of hosts."—Mal. 3:10, 11.

There it is: God says if you will bring in the tithes, He will open the windows of Heaven and pour you out a blessing. And He promises that there will be material blessings also, with larger crops and better incomes. If you believed that, you would tithe.

Again God says:

"Honour the Lord with thy substance, and with the firstfruits of all thine increase: So shall thy barns be filled with plenty, and thy presses shall burst out with new wine."—Prov. 3:9, 10.

God promises that if He gets the firstfruits of all your increase, you will have plenty of increase—with filled barns and your winepresses bursting out with grapejuice. It is a promise of material blessings because of tithing.

But Jesus says the same thing in the New Testament, in Matthew 6:33:

"But seek ye first the kingdom of God, and his righteousness; and all these things shall be added unto you."

Again in Luke 6:38, we read:

"Give, and it shall be given unto you; good measure, pressed down, and shaken together, and running over, shall men give into your bosom. For with the same measure that ye mete withal it shall be measured to you again."

God promises that with the same measure you give to Him it will be measured back to you, even material blessing. And II Corinthians 9:6 says:

"But this I say, He which soweth sparingly shall reap also sparingly; and he which soweth bountifully shall reap also bountifully."

That sowing and reaping is in material blessings. You have little money because you give little money. You are stingy with God, and God measures back to you food and clothes in the same stingy, scanty measure that you give to Him. You sow sparingly, you reap sparingly. Oh, believe me, you cannot afford *not* to tithe!

So there are many clear and definite promises in God's Word that you will be better off financially by tithing than not to tithe. He has promised to provide food and drink and clothes, if you seek first His kingdom. You cannot get ahead of God in giving. God says it, and the experiences of millions of Christians prove it so. But you do not believe it, and therefore you do not bring God the tithes and offerings!

Not to tithe proves your lack of faith and your unbelief in God and the Bible. If you think you cannot afford to tithe, then you are a modernist who does not believe the Bible!

So check up on yourself and see what kind of a Christian you are. Are you an obedient Christian, willing to do what God commands? Are you an honest Christian, paying all your obligations? Do you really love God? Are you sincerely grateful for His blessings? And do you believe His Word? In other words, are you willing to risk God to do what He said He would do?

Not until you try God out in tithes and offerings can you really answer "Yes" to these questions.

5.

JOY AND RICHES IN THE HOLY SPIRIT

Dear Christian, do not miss the blessings promised us through the Holy Spirit.

I. THE PROMISE OF THE SPIRIT

The Bible is full of great and precious promises. But for the Christian there is one promise which is so important and so oft repeated that in the language of the Saviour Himself and of the apostles, it is called, "THE PROMISE." This is the promise of the fullness of the Spirit.

Sometimes it is referred to as the baptism of the Spirit, sometimes as the gift of the Spirit, and sometimes as an enduement of power from on high, but always it has reference to the blessed power of the Holy Spirit on Christians to make them soul-winning witnesses for Christ.

This promise was given in the Old Testament when Joel was inspired to write, "And it shall come to pass afterward, that I will pour out my spirit upon all flesh" (Joel 2:28). But not much is said in the Old Testament about this promise.

It began to be clearly taught by John the Baptist. He

said, "I indeed baptize you with water unto repentance: but he that cometh after me is mightier than I, whose shoes I am not worthy to bear: he shall baptize you with the Holy Ghost, and with fire" (Matt. 3:11; Mark 1:7, 8; Luke 3:16; John 1:33). John the Baptist baptized people after they were saved. He was not talking about salvation. And he promised that Jesus would baptize people in the Holy Ghost. It was a promise of such importance that Matthew, Mark, Luke and John all were inspired to record it for us.

Jesus Repeats "The Promise"

The promise of this Holy Spirit power and fullness for soul-winning witnessing was mentioned several times by the Saviour. In John 7:37-39 we are told:

"In the last day, that great day of the feast, Jesus stood and cried, saying, If any man thirst, let him come unto me, and drink. He that believeth on me, as the scripture hath said, out of his belly shall flow rivers of living water. But this spake he of the Spirit, which they that believe on him should receive: for the Holy Ghost was not yet given; because that Jesus was not yet glorified."

Notice two things involved in this promise. The first is a promise that the Christian who believed for it and had faith for it, could have the Holy Spirit power flowing out from him like a river of water of life. Then the Scripture tells us that Jesus referred here to the Holy Spirit. God's people should expect and pray for the Holy Spirit to make them a fountain of life to all those around about them.

Another thing made clear in this passage is that the same Holy Spirit should be "received" into the bodies of Christians after the glorification, that is, the resurrection, of Jesus.

Several times in the book of John Jesus referred to the Holy Spirit as the Comforter, as one who now dwelled *with* them, but in the future should be *in* them (John 14:15-17). This Comforter was to guide them into all truth (John 16:13), to witness with them and make them witnesses (John 15:26, 27).

After the resurrection of Jesus, the same day He appeared to His disciples and breathed on them and said, "Receive ye the Holy Ghost" (John 20:22). The Holy Spirit then came in to dwell in their bodies, evidently. They "received" the Holy Ghost, as John 7:38 had said that they should receive Him.

These disciples were already saved men. Now, since the resurrection of Jesus, they had received the Holy Ghost. Besides that, the Lord Jesus opened their understanding that they should understand the Scriptures. Luke 24:45 tells us: "Then opened he their understanding, that they might understand the scriptures," after that He gave them the Great Commission and told them to go to all the world and preach the Gospel.

One would think that they were now abundantly equipped to start their soul-winning ministry, but no, the Saviour said wait. Jesus told them they were not yet ready and that their principal need was not yet filled. People cannot win souls just because they know the Bible. People cannot win souls just because God has called them to preach. No, they need a holy enduement from on high. So Jesus said to His disciples, "And, behold, I send the promise of my Father upon you: but tarry ye in the city of Jerusalem, until ye be endued with power from on high" (Luke 24:49). The Holy Spirit living in their bodies was not enough. Now He must come with a special enduement, or fullness, or baptism of soul-winning power.

Notice that Jesus said to them, "Behold, I send THE

PROMISE of my Father upon you." This promise of an enduement of power from on high is "THE PROMISE." This is the príncipal promise for a child of God. This is the main thing. This is THE equipment for soul winning. Jesus said in effect, "Do not start revivals, do not begin missionary journeys, do not begin your public testimony even in Jerusalem, until you be endued with power from on high. This is THE promise, wait for it."

In Acts again we find a word about this promise.

"And being assembled together with them, commanded them that they should not depart from Jerusalem, but wait for the promise of the Father, which, saith he, ye have heard of me. For John truly baptized with water; but ye shall be baptized with the Holy Ghost not many days hence."—Acts 1:4, 5.

Notice again that Jesus speaks of "THE PROMISE." In Luke 24:49 the promise is described as an enduement of power from on high. In Acts 1:4, 5 it is described as the baptism of the Holy Ghost. Both are the same. The baptism of the Holy Ghost is simply the fullness of power for soul winning, an enduement of power from on high.

In Acts 1:8, just below the Scripture quoted, is another word of Jesus about the blessed baptism of the Holy Ghost: "But ye shall receive power, after that the Holy Ghost is come upon you: and ye shall be witnesses unto me both in Jerusalem, and in all Judaea, and in Samaria, and unto the uttermost part of the earth."

What is the baptism of the Holy Ghost for? Is it to speak in tongues? Is it to make one sinlessly perfect? Is it to make people happy? No, no, no! It is to give people power to be witnesses for Jesus Christ. Soul-winning power is THE evidence of the baptism or filling of the Holy Ghost.

Baptism, Filling, the Gift of the Holy Ghost, and the Enduement of Power From on High Are All the Same Thing

Acts 2:4 says, "And they were filled with the Holy Ghost." It does not say they were baptized with the Holy Ghost in that passage, and yet we know that at that time the power came on them which was promised. That was the baptism of the Holy Ghost, even though it was called a filling. Actually they were not only filled but covered up, buried, baptized in the Holy Ghost. It was one and the same event. The promised baptism was a filling. The filling was the baptism. Of that there can be no doubt.

In Acts 2:16, 17, Peter told the assembled crowd that this filling of the Spirit was that pouring out of the Spirit promised by the prophet Joel. The filling of the Spirit, the pouring out of the Spirit, and the baptism of the Spirit, then, are all the same.

In Acts 2:32, 33, Peter's sermon tells us how this filling or pouring out of the Spirit was the fulfillment of "THE PROMISE."

"This Jesus hath God raised up, whereof we are all witnesses. Therefore being by the right hand of God exalted, and having received of the Father the promise of the Holy Ghost, he hath shed forth this, which ye now see and hear."

Notice again that what came at Pentecost is "THE PROMISE." This was not one of the promises, but the main promise for a Christian.

It is important to notice that THE promise did not refer to any particular outward manifestation such as the sound of a rushing mighty wind, or tongues of fire sitting on them, speaking in other languages, as they did to people in other languages, or the languages of those present, as they did at Pentecost. Outward signs were incidental. The enduement of power from on high was the thing promised. It was to make them witnesses for Jesus and give them soul-winning power.

"The Promise" Is for All Christians of Every Age

Some people believe that the baptism, or filling, or pouring out of the Holy Spirit was not for everybody but was only for those in apostolic days. Others believe that all Christians were baptized with the Holy Ghost when they were saved. Yet it seems very clear that not all Christians have the power that the disciples received at Pentecost, an enduement of power from on high. Not all Christians are powerful witnesses through the help of the Spirit.

I agree that all Christians now have the Holy Spirit dwelling in their bodies. As He came into the disciples on the day Jesus arose from the dead when He breathed on them and said, "Receive ye the Holy Ghost" (John 20:22), so now at conversion every Christian drinks in the Holy Spirit (I Cor. 12:13). He lives in the body of every Christian, as you will see from I Corinthians 3:16, 17; I Corinthians 6:19, 20; Romans 8:9; II Corinthians 6:16. The Holy Spirit has His headquarters now in the body of saved people. The Scripture clearly teaches that. But soul-winning power is another matter.

"THE PROMISE" was not for the indwelling of the Holy Spirit. "THE PROMISE" was Holy Spirit power to witness for Jesus and win souls. Every Christian has the Holy Spirit dwelling in his body. But very, very few Christians have this holy enduement of power from on high, the filling of the Spirit, or baptism of the Spirit, or gift of the Spirit (all scriptural names for the same thing).

But thank God, every Christian can have this blessed

power or fullness of the Spirit. In Acts 2:38, 39 Peter said:

"Repent, and be baptized every one of you in the name of Jesus Christ for the remission of sins, and ye shall receive the gift of the Holy Ghost. For the promise is unto you, and to your children, and to all that are afar off, even as many as the Lord our God shall call."

Notice that the promise here is not the promise of salvation alone, but again it is "the promise," the same promise of Luke 24:49; of Acts 1:4; of Acts 2:33—the promise of Holy Spirit power and fullness, the gift of the Holy Ghost.

And now comes the wonderful part of the promise. "For the promise is unto you [those present] and to your children [the Jewish race], and to all that are afar off [Gentiles as well as Jews], even as many as the Lord our God shall call [everyone who is ever saved]." The promise of the gift of the Holy Ghost is for us today, for everyone God ever called. Praise the Lord!

A careful study of the Scriptures given will convince every honest Christian that we ought to have the same soul-winning power that New Testament Christians had.

Now look at your Bibles again. In Acts 2:4, read these nine words, "And they were all filled with the Holy Ghost." Now turn to Acts 4:31 and find the same nine words, "And they were all filled with the Holy Ghost." The same crowd were filled with the Holy Ghost twice. They got the same thing after Pentecost as they got at Pentecost. They were filled with the Holy Ghost more than once. One time they had an earthquake; the other time they had the sound of a cyclone, but both times they were filled with the Holy Ghost. One time they spoke miraculously, in the languages of those present who understood and were blessed; the other time there was no one present but those of their own language and they did not speak other languages. But both times "they were all filled with the Holy Ghost." Let no one say, then, that the filling of the Holy Ghost could only come one time.

But the filling of the Holy Ghost in Acts 2:4 was the baptism of the Holy Ghost. Then the filling of the Holy Ghost in Acts 4:31 was also the baptism of the Holy Ghost. And one can be filled or baptized with the Holy Ghost, endued with power from on high, as often as he needs it. Praise the Lord, it is so for us today!

Notice again the words "filled with the Holy Ghost." Now turn to Ephesians 5:18 and you will see that is exactly what we are commanded to be, that is, to be filled with the Holy Ghost. God grant that we Christians today may claim our whole heritage and seek to be filled with the Holy Ghost so that we may win souls as Christians did in Bible times.

II. THE INDWELLING SPIRIT AND THE FULLNESS OF THE SPIRIT

Countless Christians are confused about the subject of the Holy Spirit. May every reader prayerfully read every verse of Scripture and open his heart to appreciate the one blessing that every Christian already has—the indwelling of the Spirit in his body—and to seek with all his heart the other blessing which every Christian may have and should have—the fullness of the Spirit for soul-winning power.

In a letter someone asked, "When we are born again, we are baptized with the Holy Spirit into the body of Christ, are we not? We HAVE His Spirit." Then the letter asked why some people teach that we should wait and pray for the Holy Spirit.

I think I can help all of my readers on this matter if you check these Scriptures very carefully.

Holy Spirit to Live in Christian's Body
After Christ's Resurrection

In John 7:37-39 we are told that after Jesus was glorified at His resurrection, the Holy Spirit would flow out from every Christian, that is, would make the body of a Christian His home.

"In the last day, that great day of the feast, Jesus stood and cried, saying, If any man thirst, let him come unto me and drink. He that believeth on me, as the scripture hath said, out of his belly shall flow rivers of living water. (But this spake he of the Spirit, which they that believe on him should receive: for the Holy Ghost was not yet given; because that Jesus was not yet glorified.)"

Remember that was to happen when Jesus was glorified. John 14:17 teaches the same thing. The Holy Spirit was then WITH the disciples but later would be IN them. "Even the Spirit of truth; whom the world cannot receive, because it seeth him not, neither knoweth him; but ye know him; for he dwelleth with you, and shall be in you."

In John 20:22 that promise, "and shall be in you," was fulfilled when Jesus appeared to His disciples and breathed upon them the day He rose from the dead. Romans 8:9; I Corinthians 6:19, 20; and many other passages clearly teach that every saved person now has the Holy Spirit dwelling in his body.

"But ye are not in the flesh, but in the Spirit, if so be that the Spirit of God dwell in you. Now if any man have not the Spirit of Christ, he is none of his."

"What? know ye not that your body is the temple of the Holy Ghost which is in you, which ye have of God, and ye are not your own? For ye are bought with a price:

therefore glorify God in your body, and in your spirit, which are God's."

When one is saved he is "born of the Spirit," Jesus said, and the Holy Spirit enters into his body, never to leave again. That is the indwelling of the Holy Spirit.

All Christians Buried Into the Body of Christ by the Holy Spirit at Conversion

Now you are ready to understand I Corinthians 12:13, "For by one Spirit are we all baptized into one body, whether we be Jews or Gentiles, whether we be bond or free; and have been all made to drink into one Spirit." When one is saved the Holy Spirit comes in, but that is not all. When one is saved he is buried (or baptized) into the body of Christ by the Holy Spirit. He becomes a part of the body of Christ, that body which will be caught out to meet Jesus at the Second Coming. Every saved person has been baptized into the body of Christ by the Holy Spirit.

But notice that that is an entirely different thing from being baptized with the Holy Spirit Himself. A comparison of I Corinthians 12:13 and Matthew 3:11 will show three different kinds of baptisms and that will make this matter plain in your mind.

"For by one Spirit are we all baptized into one body, whether we be Jews or Gentiles, whether we be bond or free; and have been all made to drink into one Spirit."

"I indeed baptize you with water unto repentance: but he that cometh after me is mightier than I, whose shoes I am not worthy to bear: he shall baptize you with the Holy Ghost, and with fire."

John the Baptist as an agent, baptized converts in water, the element of the burial. *Jesus baptizes* or buries

Christians in the Holy Spirit, or covers them with the Spirit. *The Holy Spirit* baptizes or buries Christians in the body of Christ. Baptism in water is done by men, baptism in the Holy Spirit is done by Jesus, and baptism into the body of Christ at salvation is done by the Holy Spirit. They are clearly three entirely separate things. It seems clear that the disciples before Pentecost were put into the body of Christ and the Holy Spirit came into their bodies to dwell. Then at Pentecost the Holy Spirit was poured out on them and they were covered or baptized with the Holy Spirit. Likewise those disciples in Acts 19:1-6. They had believed and I think they were certainly saved. If so, they were already baptized into the body of Christ by the Holy Spirit, but were not filled, covered, baptized with the Holy Spirit Himself.

According to Ephesians 4:5 there is only one literal baptism. That baptism is one kind of water baptism. But figuratively one may be said to be buried or baptized into the body of Christ, or in sufferings, or with the Holy Ghost.

It is clear that to be baptized or buried into the body of Christ by the Holy Spirit at conversion can only happen one time, for the gates of Hell cannot prevail against the church or body of Christ, and not one saved soul can prevail against the church or body of Christ, and not one saved soul can ever be taken out of that body when put into it by the Holy Spirit. To be born of the Spirit and have the Holy Spirit dwelling in one, cannot be separated from salvation, and men are saved only once.

The Filling or Baptism of the Spirit Is Different From Salvation and Being Buried Into the Body of Christ by the Spirit

But to be baptized with the Holy Spirit is a different

matter. The baptism of the Holy Ghost, promised in Acts 1:4, 5, is synonymous with the filling of the Holy Ghost which came in Acts 2:4.

"And being assembled together with them, commanded them that they should not depart from Jerusalem, but wait for the promise of the Father, which, saith he, ye have heard of me. For John truly baptized with water; but ye shall be baptized with the Holy Ghost not many days hence."

"And they were all filled with the Holy Ghost, and began to speak with other tongues, as the Spirit gave them utterance."

Read the two passages and you will see that there can be no doubt. To be filled with the Holy Ghost, to be endued with power from on high, to receive the gift of the Holy Ghost, and to be baptized with the Holy Ghost are all terms used about what happened at Pentecost. The disciples were commanded to tarry at Jerusalem until they should "be endued with power from on high" (Luke 24:49). About the same time Jesus told them to wait for the promise of the Father, for "ye shall be baptized with the Holy Ghost not many days hence" (Acts 1:5). Jesus also told them, speaking of the same promise, "But ye shall receive power after that the Holy Ghost is come upon you, and ye shall be witnesses unto me. . ." (Acts 1:8). The promise was for an enduement of power from on high, a baptism of the Holy Ghost, and power to witness, but when it came at Pentecost it was called a filling. At Pentecost when "they were all filled with the Holy Ghost," all Jesus promised was given, so the filling and the baptism are the same.

Notice also that what happened in Acts 2:4, "And they were all filled with the Holy Ghost," happened again in

Acts 4:31, "And they were all filled with the Holy Ghost." The same people could be filled (or baptized) with the Holy Ghost more than once.

Notice also this filling of the Spirit, or baptism of the Spirit, is mentioned many times as something separate from salvation and is often received after salvation. That was true, not only of the hundred and twenty at Pentecost, and the same group later, but was true of Stephen in Acts 7:55, was true of all the converts of Philip's great revival at Samaria in Acts 8:14-17, and was true of Saul, who became the Apostle Paul, in Acts 9:17 and in Acts 13:9.

It certainly is clear that New Testament Christians got something else besides salvation, and usually got it at a different time. The baptism or filling of the Holy Spirit is something that is separate and distinct from salvation. Do not be afraid of it because people sometimes speak of it, mistakenly, as a second work of grace. It is not "entire sanctification." It may be a second, third, fourth blessing, for New Testament Christians were filled again and again as they needed and sought the power of God. It is equally clear that many saved people have never been baptized or filled with the Holy Spirit. The Holy Spirit has buried them into the body of Christ and come into their bodies to dwell, but they are not filled and covered and empowered by Him for a soul-winning testimony. The fact that New Testament Christians needed to be filled again with the Spirit is proof that they were not full all the time. The disciples at Ephesus mentioned in Acts 19:1-6 did not know anything about this work of the Spirit. When the Bible commands in Ephesians 5:18, "Be filled with the Spirit," that is sufficient proof that many Christians are not filled with the Spirit.

Christians, then, should seek and secure the filling of the Holy Spirit. All Christians already have the indwelling of the Holy Spirit. You can see that the saying, "One baptism and many fillings" is not in the Bible and it does not fit in with the Bible teaching.

Conditions of the Power, Baptism, or Fullness of the Spirit

The Holy Spirit buries or baptizes one into the body of Christ when that one is saved. The condition there is simple faith in Christ for salvation. When Jesus told Nicodemus that he must be born of the Spirit, He gave John 3:16 as the way. But entirely different conditions must be met to be baptized or filled with the Holy Ghost Himself for soul-winning power. Two conditions of Holy Spirit power are mentioned in the Bible as prayer and obedience. One who wants the Holy Spirit to come upon him in fullness should ask and continue to ask. Read these Scriptures which show that prayer is essential to the power of the Holy Spirit:

"If ye then, being evil, know how to give good gifts unto your children: how much more shall your heavenly Father give the Holy Spirit to them that ask him?"—Luke 11:13.

"And, behold, I send the promise of my Father upon you: but tarry ye in the city of Jerusalem, until ye be endued with power from on high."—Luke 24:49.

The apostles obeyed the command to pray for the Holy Spirit. Acts 1:14 tells us how they prayed before Pentecost: "These all continued with one accord in prayer and supplication, with the women, and Mary the mother of Jesus, and with his brethren."

After Pentecost, the same people were filled again with the Spirit in answer to prayer. This second filling of the Spirit which the same group of people received a few days later came again as a result of prayer. Acts 4:31 tells us: "And when they had prayed, the place was shaken where they were assembled together; and they were all filled with the Holy Ghost, and they spake the word of God with boldness."

The Bible is just as clear that obedience is a condition for Holy Spirit power. In Acts 5:32, Peter said: "And we are his witnesses of these things; and so is also the Holy Ghost, whom God hath given to them that obey him."

Jesus had told the disciples before His death that the power of the Spirit would depend on their loving Him enough to keep His commandments. In John 14:15, 16, the Saviour said: "If ye love me, keep my commandments. And I will pray the Father, and he shall give you another Comforter, that he may abide with you forever."

Notice also that baptism, as obedience, is especially mentioned in connection with this gift of the Holy Ghost in Acts 2:38, 39 and in Matthew 3:16, 17. Jesus was an example to us in His baptism and finally an example in the way the Holy Spirit came on Him after baptism. This means that to obey Christ about baptism, or doing any other known duty, is necessary if we are to have the fullness or power of the Spirit in greatest measure.

We have written in detail, and I hope you will study all these Scriptures carefully. If you search out every Scripture with a prayerful heart, I am sure the Lord will help you understand His Word.

There are two great lessons I want you to get from the study of this subject. The first is that the Holy Spirit of God is in your body, and therefore you must glorify God in your body. Do not grieve the Holy Spirit by defiling His temple, your body.

The second lesson is that you may have the marvelous soul-winning power that New Testament Christians had, the fullness of the Spirit, if you meet the same requirements that they met. Most Christians are never filled with the Spirit, never have the fullness of joy and testimony and soul-winning power which is their right, for all are commanded to have it (Eph. 5:18). And you may be filled again and again every time you need it if you seek this blessing with prayerful, obedient heart.

III. PRAY FOR THE HOLY SPIRIT

In the eleventh chapter of Luke, we are told the disciples came to Jesus as He was praying in a certain place and when He had ceased, begged Him, "Lord, teach us to pray." Then He gave them the model prayer, the Lord's Prayer, with which we are familiar, and then continued with the following teaching in Luke 11:5-13:

"And he said unto them, Which of you shall have a friend, and shall go unto him at midnight, and say unto him, Friend, lend me three loaves; For a friend of mine in his journey is come to me, and I have nothing to set before him? And he from within shall answer and say, Trouble me not: the door is now shut, and my children are with me in bed; I cannot rise and give thee. I say unto you, Though he will not rise and give him, because he is his friend, yet because of his importunity he will rise and give him as many as he needeth. And I say unto you, Ask, and it shall be given you; seek and ye shall find; knock, and it shall be opened unto you. For every one that asketh receiveth; and he that seeketh findeth; and to him that knocketh it shall be opened. If a son shall ask bread of any of you that is a father, will he give him a stone? or if he ask a fish, will he for a fish give him a serpent? Or if he shall ask an egg, will he offer him a scorpion? If ye, then, being evil, know how to give good gifts unto your children: how much more shall

your heavenly Father give the Holy Spirit to them that ask him?"

The above passage is evidently intended to be a central and basic teaching on prayer. In it Jesus is answering the request of His disciples, "Lord, teach us to pray." All Scriptures are important, but this Scripture is especially so in learning how to pray.

In verses 5 to 8, quoted above, the Saviour tells us that every Christian has two friends. One is the friend who has no bread—the lost sinner. The other is the Friend who does have bread—the Lord. The obvious and central teaching of this parable is that every Christian should have bread to set before sinners, that this bread can be gotten from the Lord, and that it is only gotten by importunity. One who says, "A friend of mine in his journey is come to me, and I have nothing to set before him," tells in full the sad plight of the Christian without Holy Spirit power. That verse explains dry-eyed preaching, cold, formal churches; protracted meetings that are not revivals. That verse explains Christians who are not soul winners. None of us has bread for sinners unless we go to the other Friend who has bread and who, if we wait and plead, will rise and give us as much as we need!

Ask, Seek, and Knock

In verse 9 the Saviour said: "And I say unto you, Ask and it shall be given you; seek, and ye shall find; knock, and it shall be opened unto you." Do not overlook the connection. Jesus is still answering the request. "Lord, teach us to pray." The word "and" which starts the sentence clearly connects this promise with the importunate man who begged at midnight from one friend until he got the bread for his other friend so needy. In other words, we are to ask like that man asked, to seek like he sought, to stand at the door and knock and keep on knocking until the door is opened and we get the bread. God wants us to notice the importunity as an important element in prayer, but more especially, the importunity when begging for bread for sinners.

In verses 11 to 13 the Saviour plainly shows us that what we should pray for is the power of the Holy Spirit.

"If a son shall ask bread of any of you that is a father, will he give him a stone? or if he ask a fish, will he for a fish give him a serpent? Or if he shall ask an egg, will he offer him a scorpion? If ye then, being evil, know how to give good gifts unto your children: how much more shall your heavenly Father give the Holy Spirit to them that ask him?"

This Scripture is still talking about bread, still talking about prayer. If a child asks bread from his father, he gets bread, not a stone. How much more can the importunate man get bread from his Friend! Or in the clear words of the Saviour, "How much more shall your heavenly Father give the Holy Spirit to them that ask him?"

Verse 13 is the climax of the whole passage. Praying for the Holy Spirit is the heart of a real Christian's prayer life, when he prays as Jesus taught His disciples to pray.

There has been much confusion about this simple matter of praying for the Holy Spirit. It immediately comes to mind that saved people now have the Holy Spirit dwelling in their bodies. That is true. During the life and ministry of Jesus before His crucifixion, the Holy Spirit was with Christians, but not literally dwelling in their bodies. In John 14:17, Jesus plainly told the disciples that "he dwelleth WITH you, and shall be IN you." And now we know that the Holy Spirit lives in the body of every

Christian. "If any man have not the Spirit of Christ he is none of his" (Rom. 8:9). See also I Corinthians 6:19, 20; II Corinthians 6:16-18; I Corinthians 3:16, 17.

Actually, the change concerning the Holy Spirit's indwelling took place the day Jesus arose from the dead. In John 7:39 we are plainly told that the Holy Spirit was not even given because Jesus was not yet glorified. In John 20:22, we are told that on the day of His resurrection from the dead, the day of His glorification, Jesus breathed on the disciples and said to them, "Receive ye the Holy Ghost." That day the Holy Spirit came into the bodies of Christians everywhere as far as we can tell from the Scriptures.

Yes, it is true that the Holy Spirit already dwells in the bodies of Christians. But I want to show you that Luke 11:13 is not talking about that indwelling but about something else. When one asks for the Holy Spirit as commanded in Luke 11:13, he is not asking for an ecstasy for himself, not asking for the Holy Spirit to dwell in him. He is asking bread for the friend who has none. It is clearly a case of praying for Holy Spirit power to give the Gospel to others that Jesus had in mind when He gave the promise of Luke 11:13.

Luke and Acts Form a Consecutive Story, by the Same Author

It is important to notice that the book of Luke and the book of Acts were written by the same author. A glance at Luke 1:3 and Acts 1:1 will clearly show that one man wrote both. Both are addressed to the same person. The same Holy Spirit inspired and dictated the book of Luke and the book of Acts to the same man, Luke the physician. And the teaching about praying for the Holy Spirit in Luke 11:13 is carried right on through the book of Luke and brought to its fullness in the book of Acts.

Some are tempted to separate the two books and their teaching. Many believe that Luke 11:13 is now out of date and that that promise is not good this side of Pentecost. Many people make a dispensational change at Pentecost, which is not warranted by the Word of God. They say that before Pentecost people should have prayed for the Holy Spirit, but that He came at Pentecost and now there is no more need for a Christian to pray for Holy Spirit power. But they are mistaken. The Scripture does not warrant any such teaching. There is not a hint in the book of Luke or the book of Acts, telling the same connected story, that God anywhere changes His plan about Holy Spirit power. In fact, the Gospel of John discusses the indwelling of the Holy Spirit, but Luke discusses the soul-winning power of the Holy Spirit and so does the book of Acts. God chooses to reveal certain truths through certain authors. In the epistles and the Gospel of John, we are given the truth about the indwelling of the Holy Spirit, but in the Gospel of Luke and the book of Acts, the Lord is teaching us a different message and that is the message of soul-winning power. So we are plainly given the promise that God will give the Holy Spirit to them that ask Him, that is, Holy Spirit power.

Remember, too, that both of these books, Luke and Acts, were written this side of Pentecost, and the promise we are discussing here was recorded in the Word of God long after Pentecost. God inspired this passage in His word after Pentecost for all His people who should need Holy Spirit power after that time. Any Christian who has an unsaved friend should go to the other Friend who has plenty of bread and beg Him until He gets all the bread he needs. That teaching about the Holy Spirit fits as well now as it did that day long ago when the disciples said, "Lord, teach us to pray," and He taught them to pray for Holy Spirit power.

Praying for Holy Spirit Power Never Out of Date

This promise of the Saviour, that the heavenly Father would give the Holy Spirit to them that ask Him, was not meant for a limited time or a limited circle, as you will see if you trace it carefully through the book of Luke, then through the book of Acts. In Luke 24:49 the Saviour said,

"And, behold, I send the promise of my Father upon you: but tarry ye in the city of Jerusalem, until ye be endued with power from on high."

In Acts 1:4, 5 He repeated the command and the promise.

"And being assembled together with them, commanded them that they should not depart from Jerusalem, but wait for the promise of the Father, which, saith he, ye have heard of me. For John truly baptized with water: but ye shall be baptized with the Holy Ghost not many days hence."

In Acts 1:8 He clearly explained the result that would come when the Holy Ghost comes upon a Christian.

"But ye shall receive power, after that the Holy Ghost is come upon you: and ye shall be witnesses unto me both in Jerusalem, and in all Judaea, and in Samaria, and unto the uttermost part of the earth."

Compare this verse with the parable of the importunate man in Luke 11 and you will see that the promise of Luke 11:13 is this same Holy Ghost power, to witness for Jesus and win souls.

The promise of Luke 11:13, that the Holy Spirit would

be given to those that ask for Him, was fulfilled in several cases in the book of Acts. Let us consider them here.

1. AT PENTECOST. In Acts 1:14 we are told how the disciples prayed for Holy Spirit power before Pentecost: "These all continued with one accord in prayer and supplication, with the women, and Mary the mother of Jesus, and with his brethren."

Notice the word "supplication." That is what the importunate man did when he was begging for bread for his hungry friend. Supplication and the importunity are the same, and that is what we should do if we want the Holy Spirit power. The second chapter of Acts tells how wonderfully that prayer of several days' time was answered, and the Holy Spirit came upon the disciples in great power. "And they were all filled with the Holy Ghost" (Acts 2:4). The Father gave the Holy Ghost to those who asked Him.

It is important to notice, too, that the filling of the Holy Ghost did not begin at Pentecost. Many times before this, people were filled with the Holy Ghost. This same divinely inspired author, Luke, tells of several such cases. John the Baptist was "filled with the Holy Ghost, even from his mother's womb" (Luke 1:15). "Elisabeth was filled with the Holy Ghost" (Luke 1:41). "Zacharias was filled with the Holy Ghost" (Luke 1:67). (Incidentally, it is interesting to notice that Luke discusses the filling of the Holy Spirit, and that John, who discusses the indwelling of the Holy Spirit, does not anywhere use the term "filled with the Holy Ghost."

But what I want you to see here is that the filling of the Spirit did not begin at Pentecost. The indwelling of the Spirit began at the resurrection of Christ, but that is another matter entirely. As the filling of the Holy Spirit did not begin at Pentecost, then we should not expect it to end there. Luke 11:13 was good before Pentecost and was good at Pentecost. We shall see it is still good for us since Pentecost.

2. DISCIPLES AFTER PENTECOST. In the 4th chapter of Acts, Peter and John had been imprisoned, and then after being threatened, they returned to their company and all had a season of prayer, praying for boldness and power. Then, Acts 4:31 tells us, "And when they had prayed, the place was shaken where they were assembled together; AND THEY WERE ALL FILLED WITH THE HOLY GHOST and they spake the word of God with boldness."

Here it was after Pentecost, and the disciples received the Holy Spirit power by prayer! It was still true that "how much more shall your heavenly Father give the Holy Spirit to them that ask him?"

3. THE CONVERTS AT SAMARIA. In the 8th chapter of Acts, Philip went down to Samaria and had a great revival, and many converts. But these converts had not received the Holy Spirit. Acts 8:14-17 tells us:

"Now when the apostles which were at Jerusalem heard that Samaria had received the word of God, they sent unto them Peter and John: Who, when they were come down, prayed for them, that they might receive the Holy Ghost: (For as yet he was fallen upon none of them: only they were baptized in the name of the Lord Jesus). Then laid they their hands on them, and they received the Holy Ghost."

How did these new converts receive the Holy Ghost? Through prayer! The apostles came and prayed for them. Doubtless they themselves united in the prayer. At Pentecost and in Acts 4:31, people had united in prayer and been filled with the Spirit. Here again, in answer to prayer, God had kept His promise and given the Holy Spirit.

4. PAUL FILLED WITH THE SPIRIT. The Apostle Paul was converted on the road to Damascus. There he met Jesus, called Him Lord, said, "Lord, what wilt thou have me to do?" received his commission to preach the Gospel, and was led down to Damascus. But Paul, though converted, had not been filled with the Holy Spirit. In Acts 9:11 the Lord told Ananias to go to the house of Judas and enquire "for one called Saul, of Tarsus: for, behold he PRAYETH." Paul was praying, and Acts 9:9 tells us that for three days Paul "neither did eat nor drink."

The Lord convinced Ananias that Paul was saved, and verse 17 tells us, "And Ananias went his way, and entered into the house; and putting his hands on him said, Brother Saul, the Lord, even Jesus, that appeared unto thee in the way as thou camest, hath sent me, that thou mightest receive thy sight, and be filled with the Holy Ghost."

Paul was already "Brother Saul," a saved man, but the Lord sent Ananias that he might "BE FILLED WITH THE HOLY GHOST." The point is that Paul fasted and prayed three days and nights, and then received the Holy Ghost. With Paul that blessed promise of Luke 11:13 was true, that "how much more shall your heavenly Father give the Holy Spirit to them that ask him?"

Christians, Try It!

Bible Christians believed the promise of Jesus that the heavenly Father would give the Holy Spirit to those that asked Him. They asked before Pentecost, and the Holy Spirit was given in the second chapter of Acts. And again they prayed, and Acts 4:31 tells us that they were all filled with the Holy Ghost again. Peter and John went down to

Samaria and prayed for them that they might receive the Holy Ghost, and they did. Then Paul, the new convert, tried the promise. He asked the heavenly Father, prayed three days and nights with fasting, importunity and supplication, and then he too was filled with the Holy Spirit.

A Christian can have many things without begging for them. Often God answers before we call. He gives a thousand blessings which we do not even ask for. And a lost sinner can always instantly get the ear of God if he sincerely and penitently asks for salvation. Whosoever shall call upon the name of the Lord shall be saved.

But this matter of Holy Spirit power to win many souls comes only to those who earnestly ask, seek and knock. That Friend who had the bread did not arise and give him because he was his friend. He only did it because of his importunity.

If you want Holy Spirit power, if you want bread for hungry, unsaved friends, then you may have it, but you may have it only the same way that Bible Christians had it—and that is by prayer and supplication.

6.

JOY IN WELL-REARED CHILDREN

"Correct thy son, and he shall give thee rest; yea, he shall give delight unto thy soul."—Prov. 29:17.

"Children, obey your parents in the Lord: for this is right. Honour thy father and mother; which is the first commandment with promise; That it may be well with thee, and thou mayest live long on the earth. And, ye fathers, provoke not your children to wrath: but bring them up in the nurture and admonition of the Lord."—Eph. 6:1-4.

Of the Ten Commandments, the first four show man's duty to God, and the remaining six show man's duty to man. Of these latter, the first command is "Honour thy father and thy mother" (Exod. 20:12). Of a child's duty to all mankind, his first obligation is to honor his father and mother. In the order given by divine inspiration, his duty is first to his father and then to his mother, and to honor the father and mother is placed before the commands not to kill, nor commit adultery, nor steal, nor lie.

Thus the duty of children to obey their parents is one of the basic fundamentals of all human duties. God Himself calls this "the first commandment with promise," and the wonderful promise is "that it may be well with thee, and that thou mayest live long on the earth." Where children obey their parents and where sons and daughters honor their fathers and mothers, the homes will prosper and be blessed and happy. Men and women will have been trained to be industrious and honest and obedient to authority. In such a land, we may be sure that schools and churches and government will be blessed of God. Therefore this command is the first with a promise.

So the command as stated above is restated in the New Testament: "Children, obey your parents in the Lord: for this is right." In Colossians 3:20 the command is even stronger, "Children, obey your parents in all things: for this is well pleasing unto the Lord."

Sons and daughters should honor their father and their mother. This does not mean that little children should simply obey their parents, but that grown men and women should care for their aged parents and respect them and honor them. Jesus rebuked the Pharisees strongly because by their tradition they allowed a man to say, "It is Corban," and then refuse to do any more to support his mother and father (Mark 7:9-13). Jesus plainly told them that they thus violated the command, "Honour thy father and thy mother." So to honor one's father and mother means to support them in their old age as well as when children. They are to obey them and, when adults, to revere and respect them.

"And, ye fathers, provoke not your children to wrath," says God's Word in Ephesians 6:4. I think fathers need this command more than mothers. At any rate, it is given in similar words in Colossians 3:21, "Fathers, provoke not your children to anger, lest they be discouraged." In the average modern home, the father is not counted so important, perhaps, but in homes of Bible Christians, the father was a real person to be respected. His rebuke was taken to heart. His authority was strong. Fathers are warned not to provoke their children to wrath.

Discipline is always hard. In the language of Scripture, "No chastening for the present seemeth to be joyous, but grievous." There is plenty of instruction about disciplining children and the Scriptures are very strong. But first of all, here fathers are cautioned that the results of discipline should not be disheartening and discouraging. The proper discipline of children will not leave them angry at the parents but penitent and affectionate.

I read once an article in a popular magazine in which a woman journalist declared fervently that had her mother or father ever whipped her, she would have hated them! Unfortunately, she had never had what she needed as a child or she would not talk and write in such a way. Chastening does not seem joyous, but "it yieldeth the peaceable fruit of righteousness unto them which are exercised thereby," the Scripture says, and that is true about our own children as well as God's children, provided we correct them in the spirit which is commanded in Ephesians 6:4.

Children Need "Bringing Up"

The command about children is to "bring them up in the nurture and admonition of the Lord." Children are to be brought up, to be reared. If they are left like Topsy, a little Negro girl in "Uncle Tom's Cabin," who "just growed," they will not turn out well. The Scripture tells us, "A child left to himself bringeth his mother to shame" (Prov. 29:15). Any father and mother who have a child, have a job on their hands, for God commands that that child be brought up. Children do not simply "turn out" well or poorly by their parents. In this matter, God puts the responsibility on the parents and not on the child.

In Proverbs 22:6 we are told, "Train up a child in the way he should go: and when he is old, he will not depart from it." Children do not train themselves up, do not bring themselves up, do not discipline themselves, do not automatically grow into good characters. When children grow into good men and women, it is because they have been brought up that way.

For this reason, God gives us children nearly twenty years before they grow up. God meant, then, that it should take some twenty years of hard work on the part of the father and mother to set and grow and nurture and correct the character of the children, to make them the kind of men and women they ought to be. A hog, bigger than man, gets grown in a year, a cow in two years, and a horse in about three. God knew that children needed bringing up.

Notice that this command is given primarily to fathers. Every father is responsible for the rearing of the children; more responsible than is the mother. God set men to head the homes and families. They must account to Him for the rearing or bringing up of their children.

Joshua and Abraham Recognized Their Responsibility for Their Children

Many great characters in the Bible acknowledged their responsibility for their children. Joshua, in his last oration to the elders, heads, judges and officers of the tribes and families of Israel, boldly declared, "As for me and my house, we will serve the Lord!" (Josh. 24:15). Joshua was willing to speak for his wife and for his children. He himself would serve the Lord and he would see that his family served the Lord. He knew that he could not avoid the responsibility before God and so he exercised it.

God commended Abraham that he ruled well over his

family. God did not hide from Abraham His plans for the destruction of Sodom, but He said, "For I know him, that he will command his children and his household after him, and they shall keep the way of the Lord, to do justice and judgment." Abraham ruled his family well and did it by command. His children and his household were "brought up" in the nurture and admonition of the Lord. Fathers must bring up their children.

Because Eli failed in this matter of discipline and the bringing up of his sons, God put a curse on his whole priestly family. In I Samuel 2:29 God asked Eli, "Wherefore kick ye at my sacrifice and at mine offering, which I have commanded in my habitation; and honourest thy sons above me, to make yourself fat with the chiefest of all the offerings of Israel my people?" In I Samuel 3:13 God said concerning Eli, "For I have told him that I will judge his house for ever for the iniquity which he knoweth: because his sons made themselves vile, and he restrained them not." God holds fathers accountable to restrain their sons, to discipline them, to correct them and bring them up.

In the New Testament special commands are given to preachers. In I Timothy 3:4, we are told that the pastor should be "one that ruleth well his own house, having his children in subjection with all gravity." To bring up children means to rule them well and have them in subjection with all gravity. In verse 12, we are told that deacons should be "ruling their children and their own houses well." In Titus 1:6 Paul is inspired to command that an elder must have "faithful children not accused of riot or unruly." A man who has unruly children is not bringing them up right and is not fit to be a pastor. One sees the importance of bringing up children well from this command.

In a revival at Sentinel, Oklahoma, years ago, I was distressed because, although when I visited store after store in the town inviting people to come to the revival, they were very courteous to me but few ever came. I could not understand their lack of confidence and interest until one night about 2:00 a.m. the pastor's 19-year-old son came home drunk, could not get in the locked door, and was found sleeping in his vomit in the church basement the next day. Good men did not trust the leadership of a pastor whose influence for God could not save his own son from gross sin. There is some serious lack when a pastor cannot claim Proverbs 22:6 for his children, "Train up a child in the way he should go: and when he is old, he will not depart from it."

The "Nurture of the Lord"

Fathers are to bring up their children "in the nurture and admonition of the Lord." The word nurture here means instruction or chastening. It is translated once in the Bible as "instruction," three times as "chastening," and once as "chastisement." In Hebrews 12:5, 7 and 11 the word chastening means correction, and each time the original Greek word is the same as this one translated "nurture" in Ephesians 6:4. In Hebrews 12:8, "chastisement" is translated from the same Greek word as translated here, "nurture." In II Timothy 3:16 the same Greek word is translated "instruction."

It is clear, then, that when fathers are commanded to bring up their children in the nurture of the Lord, they are to bring them up with chastening and chastisement, as God deals with His children. The inescapable idea is that children must be taught to obey and must be punished for wrongdoing in such a way as to discipline them, correct their faults and establish their character.

Should Parents Whip Children?

Is corporal punishment for children required in the Bible? It most certainly is! And the teaching is so clear that every parent must acknowledge it. There can be no material difference of opinion on this matter by honest believers in the Word of God.

Sin must be punished. That is the teaching throughout the Bible. Under the Mosaic law detailed instructions were given for the punishment of specific sins. In the New Testament we are told that rulers are the ministers of God to execute wrath. Sin must be punished and God Himself will certainly see that it is eventually punished. The doctrine of punishment for sin is unpopular with many. They do not like the punishment of criminals by the state nor the punishment of sinners in Hell nor the punishment of children by the parents. But sin must be judged and punished, and the parent is accountable to God to judge and punish the sins of his children. Children are to be brought up in the nurture or chastening and admonition of the Lord.

The book of Proverbs has a wealth of instructions for practical daily living, and the Proverbs given are a part of the inspired Word of God. Read these plain commands there to whip children.

1. Proverbs 13:24: "He that spareth his rod hateth his son; but he that loveth him chasteneth him betimes."

The worldly-minded parent, to excuse his sin in not punishing his child, may say, "I love him too much." That is a foolish excuse and untrue. "He that spareth the rod hateth his son; but he that loveth him chasteneth him betimes," that is, pretty often. One who doesn't whip his children may love his own ease. It is not easy to enforce discipline whether in home, school, or government, but it is wise and it is for the welfare of those governed, always.

The parent who does not chastise his child does not have the best interest of the child at heart, and brings evil on the child.

2. Proverbs 19:18: "Chasten thy son while there is hope, and let not thy soul spare for his crying."

God gave long years in which to rear children. While they are young and tender in years, "there is hope" that is, they may be made into the kind of men and women that you desire if you begin early and enforce the right and punish their sins. Whip your son and daughter while there is hope, for a little later it will be too late. Multitudes of careless parents have found this Scripture true to their everlasting sorrow.

You hate to hear your children cry. But how much more you will grieve to see their sorrows later in life, brought on by sins that were not rebuked in childhood!

Do not withhold the rod of correction because children cry. Do not stop whipping as soon as they start crying, God says. The divinely inspired wisdom of the book of Proverbs commands us to punish our children while it will be effective, considering, not their immediate pain but their future and permanent welfare.

My father had a rule that he regularly followed when he punished us. He whipped until we cried and then whipped until we stopped! And none of the eight children ever thought my father rash or bitter. He did not provoke his children to wrath, but he did bring us up in the nurture or chastening of the Lord. He chastened us while there was hope and he did not spare the rod because of our crying.

3. Proverbs 20:30: "The blueness of a wound cleanseth away evil: so do stripes the inward parts of the belly."

How detailed and careful are the commands of God on this matter! The rule of a father must sometimes be severe. Punishment must sometimes be drastic. If you consider scores of incidents in the Bible and see how drastic the punishments of God were for seemingly small offenses, you will understand this rule.

Achan and his whole family were stoned to death for the theft of a wedge of gold, some silver, and a Babylonian garment. A man was stoned, by direct command of God, for picking up sticks on the Sabbath. The Amalekites were to be destroyed—men, women, children and cattle—because of their idolatry and their opposition to God and His people, Israel. The thought of Hell itself is a terrible thought. It must impress you that terrible and drastic punishment for sin must sometimes be administered.

So here parents are encouraged by the statement that "the blueness of a wound cleanseth away evil" and that "so do stripes the inward parts of the belly." Children should sometimes be whipped until there are stripes on their bodies. If this seems to be wrong, then you do not have the attitude you ought to have toward the Word of God and, very likely, you have not reared children thoroughly and successfully according to the Bible pattern.

Every good parent grieves when he must punish a child painfully. The old saying, "This hurts me more than it does you," has been joked about a great deal, but it is a tearful and sad fact known by multitudes of fathers and mothers who honestly punish their children as the Bible commands. To do what the Bible commands is not easy, but it is certainly profitable and happy in its fruits.

I never will forget the first time I whipped one of my children until blue marks appeared on her fat little body. She had been stubborn and rebellious and I had to spank her several times for the same thing before I got results. Eventually I did the job so thoroughly that she surrendered and obeyed me, though my own heart was torn and grieved beyond expression. I could not keep back the tears later when I saw the tiny stripes or marks left by my spanking. Since that time she has left black and blue marks a hundred times on her body in her play, but no other marks ever did her so much good!

According to the Scripture, "stripes" cleanse "the inward parts of the belly." Happy is the child that has been so earnestly chastised by the loving hands of a mother and father that the selfish natural will of the child was surrendered to the higher and better will of the father and mother. Stripes left by such chastisement cleanse the innermost parts of the belly, according to the Word of God. This may not fit in with the carnal teachings of men, but God knows more about rearing children than psychology professors in all the colleges, and all the old maids who write columns for mothers in the newspapers!

4.   Proverbs 22:15: "Foolishness is bound in the heart of a child; but the rod of correction shall drive it far from him."

The human race is foolish by nature, and folly, as used in the Bible, refers to wickedness. Our children are wicked by nature. They were born of wicked parents. Every little baby born in this world inherits the taint of sin. Do not misunderstand me; little children are not lost sinners. They are kept safe, I believe, by the blood of Jesus Christ. Whatever was lost in Adam's sin has been regained for unaccountable children by the death of Christ. But every child has inborn characteristics that will make him a deliberate, wilful sinner as soon as he comes to the place and power of choice.

A child only a few days old can get very angry. As soon as he learns to talk, a child begins to lie. To steal is as natural for him as to eat. And every child would rather take the toys that belong to another than not; so the opposite course must be drilled into him by rebuke and punishment.

According to the Bible, "Foolishness is bound in the heart of a child." There is something terribly evil and wicked in the nature of every human being and that will only be brought into subjection and driven out by punishment. "The rod of correction shall drive it far from him."

That does not mean that people can be saved by the development of character or that sin can be entirely overcome by training. It takes the blood of Christ to save. But it does mean that every child can be disciplined, corrected and trained until he will have a strong and sturdy moral character which he will not have who grows up without discipline and the rod of correction.

Whipping has a very definite place and purpose in God's plan for rearing children.

5. Proverbs 23:13, 14: "Withhold not correction from the child: for if thou beatest him with the rod, he shall not die. Thou shalt beat him with the rod, and shall deliver his soul from hell."

The fond mother is likely to believe that her husband, the child's father, is killing the little fellow. But the Bible says, "If thou beat him with a rod, he shall not die." Punishment should always be in the fear of God and as a matter of principle. Certainly it is never right to punish children as a matter of personal spite or in uncontrolled anger. God loves sinners and punishes them, yea, He punishes His own children and in the same spirit and for the same purpose Christian parents should punish their children when necessary. To whip a child may mean the eternal salvation of his soul and it may keep him out of Hell. "Thou shalt beat him with the rod, and shall deliver his soul from hell." Doubtless thousands of people are now in Hell who would have been saved had they been reared as they ought to have been, brought up in the nurture or chastening and admonition of the Lord.

In my father's home the children were all converted young. It was never hard for us to believe that sin must be punished, for at our house sin was punished with love but with faithfulness. It was not hard for us to believe that God was kind and merciful, for our father too was kind and merciful and grieved when it was necessary to punish.

The child who had been taught to reverence his father and mother and obey them is much more easily taught to reverence and obey God. One who sees that sin must be punished is much quicker to confess and forsake his sins.

One who whips his child may save his soul from Hell!

6. Proverbs 29:15: "The rod and reproof give wisdom: but a child left to himself bringeth his mother to shame."

There is an old saying, "Experience is a dear school, but fools will learn in no other." Yet it is a sad fact that many people do not learn by experience. The pupils in the school of experience need a teacher to point out the moral. So the Bible says, "The rod and reproof give wisdom." There can be no real spiritual wisdom until a child learns the self-control, reverence and obedience to authority and the anxiety to do right which comes by the punishment for wrongdoing. Many a wise man today will testify that the rod and reproof of a godly father and mother gave wisdom in his boyhood.

"But a child left to himself bringeth his mother to shame." Rearing children is a serious business. God did not mean that children should boss in their home. God did not mean that children should make their own choices in everything. Children need supervision, advice, admonition and correction. Many a heartbroken mother has told me how her boy was then in the penitentiary because of some shocking crime. Every such case proves the rule laid down in the Word of God, that "a child left to himself bringeth his mother to shame."

7. Proverbs 29:17: "Correct thy son, and he shall give thee rest; yea, he shall give delight unto thy soul."

It is a happy thing for a man in his old age to have his sons and daughters, fine godly men and women, about him or doing a great work in the world. Such children give delight to their parents. They honor and support their parents in their old age. Such children give rest to the souls of the mother and father who reared them right. The father and mother who punish their children and make them mind will have a long harvest of happiness as they delight in the character that they helped develop and enjoy the fruits of the correction of their children.

The importance of the discipline of children and the insisting of absolute obedience is clearly shown in Deuteronomy 21:18-21. There the Jews were commanded that if a man had a stubborn and rebellious son who would not obey his mother or father and after they had whipped him, he would not listen, then he was to be taken before the elders of the city where he would be condemned and then carried outside the city and stoned. Discipline is much more important, as taught in the Bible, than is generally held by Christians.

May God help us to rear our children in the nurture and admonition of the Lord and so avoid the terrible disaster that comes to a lawless people. Disobedience in the home will mean lawless citizens of the state and rebels against God later on.

"The Admonition of the Lord"

Fathers are to bring up their children "in the nurture and admonition of the Lord." The word "nurture" is translated "instruction" in one case which I mentioned above. And the term "admonition" means just that and is so translated the three times it is used in the New Testament.

There is far more, then, to bringing up children than just whipping them. Correction is a very important matter, but so also is admonition or instruction or counsel. The father is to teach his children.

In Deuteronomy 6:6-9 Jewish fathers were commanded to diligently instruct their children. There Moses was inspired to say:

"And these words, which I command thee this day, shall be in thine heart: And thou shalt teach them diligently unto thy children, and shalt talk of them when thou sittest in thine house, and when thou walkest by the way, and when thou liest down, and when thou risest up. And thou shalt bind them for a sign upon thine hand, and they shall be as frontlets between thine eyes. And thou shalt write them upon the posts of thy house, and on thy gates."

Parents were to teach the Scriptures "diligently" to their children. They were to talk to their children about the commands of God as they sat in the house and when they walked by the way and at bed time and again when they arose in the morning! The words of God were to be bound upon the hand of the father and as frontlets between his eyes, and the father was to write the great commandment to love God with all the heart, mind and soul on the posts of his house and on his gates! Parents ought diligently to teach their children about God and His commandments.

Similar commands were repeated in Deuteronomy 11:18-20.

When Joshua led the children of Israel over the River Jordan and into the land of Canaan, the people carried rocks from the midst of the River Jordan and piled them up in Gilgal (Josh. 4:6). Then each father was commanded to instruct his children concerning the mighty deeds of God. When children would ask the question, "What mean these stones?" the fathers were to tell them of all the marvelous deeds God had done for His people, including the crossing of the River Jordan.

Timothy grew into a great preacher of the Gospel and that is not surprising, considering the teaching he had as a child. Paul wrote to Timothy, "I thank God. . .when I call to remembrance the unfeigned faith that is in thee, which dwelt first in thy grandmother Lois, and thy mother Eunice; and I am persuaded that in thee also"(II Tim. 1:3, 5). A part of Timothy's faith was a spiritual inheritance from his mother and his grandmother, good women who reared him and taught him the Word of God. Again Paul reminded Timothy "that from a child thou hast known the holy scriptures which are able to make thee wise unto salvation through faith which is in Christ Jesus." Happy, fortunate Timothy! In his childhood his mother had taught him the Scriptures that told of the plan of salvation. I am sure that Timothy never sowed the wild oats that have broken the heart of other mothers and fathers. He was brought up in the nurture and admonition of the Lord.

Win Your Children to Christ

Fathers and mothers should win their own children to Christ. No one else is so well fitted or so responsible for winning them.

Jesus said, "Suffer little children to come unto me and forbid them not for of such is the kingdom of heaven." Parents often stand in the way of their children. To the mother, her ten-year-old boy is still "only a baby." She is so afraid that "he doesn't understand." But likely he does understand, too, that he is a sinner and that he needs Christ. Certainly if he is normal in mind and has been properly taught, he will understand that he needs salvation. No age limit can be set, but parents often sin in that they do not carefully watch or that they carelessly hinder their children.

Dear Father, Mother, permit your children to seek Christ, yea, encourage them to. God wants little children to be saved.

"SUFFER little children." I never fully knew what that meant until just now. I have looked it up carefully and the Greek word translated "suffer" also means "to send away," "let go," "permit." Not only should parents permit their children to come to Christ, but they should "send them away" to Christ, that is, urge them to go. Twice in the New Testament the word here translated "suffer" is translated "send away."

Every parent is responsible for the conversion of his child. You ought to have more influence than anybody over that dear one who is part of your own flesh and bones. Do not neglect your opportunity, but bring up your children in the nurture and admonition of the Lord. And part of that admonition will be in urging upon them to trust Jesus as Saviour and love Him and serve Him.

7.

JOY ON A SICKBED

I. HOW GOD BROUGHT BLESSING BEYOND PRICE IN SICKNESS

"The Lord will strengthen him upon the bed of languishing: thou wilt make all his bed in his sickness."—Ps. 41:3.

Some years ago this writer was sick, and when I get sick that is something to write home about. For many, many years I have had an iron constitution. By the mercy of God I have been unusually strong all my days. For that I devoutly thank God. I thank Him all the more for it when I consider how unusual have been His mercies to me in this respect.

That Sunday afternoon, in Dallas, Texas, I became ill enough that I found it would be dangerous, if not impossible, to continue without going to bed. Sunday morning my large class had been very happy and then at 11:00 o'clock what a time of tears and heart-searching God gave us! God had led me to preach on "The Call of Isaiah and the Absolute Surrender." I laid much stress on the cleansing fire of the coal from the altar and on the surrendered will. It was with very real regret that I felt compelled to miss the radio service and the evening sermon and the happy jubilee hour which had become so precious to many of us. But I went to bed and turned the service over to my assistant pastor.

"Satan Hath Desired to Have You, That He May Sift You As Wheat"

For several months I had been under bombardment from Satan. Jesus told Peter, "Satan hath desired to have you, that he may sift you as wheat: But I have prayed for thee, that thy faith fail not." Satan desired Job to tempt and try him. Doubtless, Satan often selects individuals, particularly preachers whom God uses, to break down, if possible, their faith and their testimony.

It began in betrayal and heartless, wicked attack by former friends. Satan desperately tried to block a city wide revival, but God gave us grace. When doors seemed to be closed, yet we went forward boldly and they opened again and again just in time. God gave a marvelous revival.

Next, the Devil tried me sorely in attempting to disrupt and split our church. All true pastors love their churches, but someway I feel that I have carried these in my bosom as a nursing father, even as Moses felt about the children of Israel. They were my little sheep; my lambs; my babes in Christ. So many of them I had gotten by travail of soul. Hundreds of them I baptized with these two hands. In scores of cases I led them first into soul winning, and I was allowed of God to really unfold to them the Scriptures. They loved me and I loved them. If Satan could have broken up the Fundamentalist Baptist Church in Dallas, he would have broken my heart, as he well knew. Now God had brought to naught the wicked efforts of those who sought to ruin the church. The spirit, harmony, attendance, offerings and fellowship are greater, if possible, than ever before. Several hundred professed faith in Christ that year and we baptized nearly every Sunday. Thank God for victory.

The trials mentioned did not originate with men, but I believe from Satan. So it was not surprising to me that the Evil One should attack my health. I worked long hours day in and day out for many months. The strain of great revivals, our building program, preparing copy for THE SWORD, had been very heavy. I had preached daily straight on through a rather severe attack of flu. Kidney trouble appeared and then other complications, now I was on my back.

The Blessing of Sickness

Several Scriptures had been very sweet to me in this time of sickness. I thank God that He assured me from the very beginning that this sickness was to His glory and to my good. Psalm 41:3 was certainly true in my case.

"The Lord will strengthen him upon the bed of languishing: thou wilt make all his bed in his sickness."

A thousand blessings were showered upon me on my sickbed.

First of these, God definitely and clearly answered prayer at a very definite time. He spoke to me and took away the pain which had been most severe. He gave me sweet assurance, then impressed me that He had taken the case in hand, and in the evening of the same day the fever of 103.4 left. Since then there was not a moment but that I was certain the Lord had the case in hand and had definitely answered prayer. The prayers of hundreds in my behalf were heard, and one group at least was in a season of prayer at the very time the answer came. Doctors and medicines proved themselves incidentals. It was good to be sick, to prove again that God answers prayer.

Another blessing of sickness is the sweetness of friendship. Before me on the dresser, tall lilies reared their lovely heads and spread the perfume from their creamy pistils. Beside them, another vase held orange-red Texas plumes, climbing high, like the lilies. On another table a great armful of larkspears, sent by loving hands, gladdened the sickroom for days. Elsewhere in the room tiger lilies and roses told of the love of friends, and better, of the love of God! For many years I had been too busy for flowers except for an instant glance or smell. Now I rejoiced in their fragrance. And I rejoiced in the fragrance of friends.

Many people came by the scores to tell me they were praying for me, or they sent me word. Some came into my room too broken up to speak and with tears of compassion. One said, "I wish it could be me sick and you could be well." Dozens knelt by my bed and prayed. From all over the city had come word from members and friends and even strangers, saying that they prayed for my speedy recovery.

The Sick Room, a Place of Blessing

Brother W. W. C———— phoned one night and asked permission to bring a troubled friend to my room that I might pray for him. With his wife he came and with them a man and his wife. The man had long been away from God, out of duty, cold and wicked. He said, "I want to get right with God, but I can't. I need help." So I read the Bible awhile and I suggested that we pray. They knelt around my bed and one after another of us prayed. Finally the poor troubled backslider prayed to have mercy and forgiveness and peace and victory. He prayed, "O God, if You will give me again the joy of my salvation, I will never leave You again as long as I live!" Right there on his knees he got the blessing he wanted and needed, and so that Sunday morning he and his wife and daughter joined our church for baptism and I baptized them.

But the sweetest blessing of being sick, I found in my own heart. I had time to meditate, and meditation was sweet. One night when my head was burning with fever and I tossed nearly all night through, I kept thinking of the hands of Jesus. They were carpenter's hands, worn, work-hardened hands. They were gentle hands, too, for He laid them on the heads of the sick and they recovered, and with them He blessed little children. With the fingers He mixed the spittle and clay that healed the eyes of a blind man. They were merciful, tender hands.

Again, I mused throughout the night—they were mighty hands, the hands of a God. The safety of every born-again child depends on those hands. Jesus said, "No man can pluck them out of my hands." And best of all (I saw them a hundred times that night!), they were wounded hands, with the nail scars, the hands of a Saviour. It is good to be sick if we see and feel the hands of Christ!

One day I had one of the girls read to me twice those last two wonderful chapters in the Bible about the Heavenly Jerusalem. It was never so sweet to me before. I noticed that the Bible did not call the new Jerusalem "beautiful" or "wonderful" or "magnificent" or "superb" or "marvelous." Those words are all too little, too puny to picture that Heavenly city! Not an adjective is used in describing the gates, each one of which is a separate pearl! The only time the word "great" is used is in the sense of large—the walls were great, that is, large and high. I learned that the beauties of the Heavenly Jerusalem must be taught by the Holy Spirit, for "Eye hath not seen, nor ear heard, neither have entered into the heart of man, the things which God hath prepared for them that love him.

But God hath revealed them unto us by his Spirit" (I Cor. 2:9, 10). So as I mused the fire burned, and as I lay there on this bed with an aching back and a burning skin, God talked to my heart and I talked straight to the heart of Him. I walked in boldly to a throne of grace to find mercy to help in time of need and I got it.

Do not be afraid of the fires of cleansing. A loving father chastens every son whom He loves, and according to the Scripture, He "makes all his bed in his sickness." This bed of sickness was of God and so I embraced it and loved it. I did not resent it nor fear it. I had no anxiety about it. If it was of God, it was good, for I am His and He loves me.

The sickbed is not easy. It was particularly hard for me at first. When the pain was at its worst and when God seemed not to have answered, then it was hard to be patient and hard to trust. It must have been so with Job when his wife said, "Curse God and die," and when his three friends accused him and argued with him. But I took counsel from the sufferings of the saints and tried to follow the words of the Scriptures in James 5:10, 11:

"Take, my brethren, the prophets, who have spoken in the name of the Lord, for an example of suffering affliction, and of patience. Behold, we count them happy which endure. Ye have heard of the patience of Job, and have seen the end of the Lord; that the Lord is very pitiful, and of tender mercy."

Let us remember that God always has an end in view, and remember "the end of the Lord; that the Lord is very pitiful, and of tender mercy."

The whole 41st Psalm is precious to me and so I quote it here:

"Blessed is he that considereth the poor: the Lord will deliver him in time of trouble.

The Lord will preserve him, and keep him alive, and he shall be blessed upon the earth; and thou wilt not deliver him unto the will of his enemies.

The Lord will strengthen him upon the bed of languishing: thou wilt make all his bed in his sickness.

I said, Lord, be merciful unto me: heal my soul; for I have sinned against thee.

Mine enemies speak evil of me. When shall he die, and his name perish?

And if he come to see me, he speaketh vanity: his heart gathereth iniquity to itself; when he goeth abroad, he telleth it.

All that hate me whisper together against me: against me do they devise my hurt.

An evil disease, say they, cleaveth fast unto him: and now that he lieth he shall rise up no more.

Yea, mine own familiar friend, in whom I trusted, which did eat of my bread, hath lifted up his heel against me.

But thou, O Lord, be merciful unto me, and raise me up, that I may requite them.

By this I know that thou favourest me, because mine enemy doth not triumph over me.

And as for me, thou upholdest me in mine integrity, and settest me before thy face for ever.

Blessed be the Lord God of Israel from everlasting, and to everlasting, Amen, and Amen."

Let all those who have found that God strengthens the languishing and that "he makes all his bed in his sickness" say with me and with the psalmist, "Amen, and Amen."

II. GOD HEALS THE SICK IN ANSWER TO PRAYER

In Dallas, Texas, in 1935, I had a wonderful experience

of answered prayer and wrote of it for THE SWORD OF THE LORD.

I have had other such remarkable answers to prayer for healing. For example, in 1932 I prayed for a woman after she had spent two years in a state sanitarium for T.B. patients at Kerrville, Texas, and came home to die. She was marvelously healed; in two weeks she was doing all her own housework, and for more than thirty years has had no recurrence of the dread disease.

But one example is worth a thousand arguments so I quote for you the testimony I wrote long ago, in 1935.

Brother J. A. Middleton Is Wonderfully Healed

Near the first of March, Brother J. A. Middleton, an earnest Christian man, and treasurer of the Fundamentalist Baptist Tabernacle in Dallas, was taken seriously and dangerously ill. He was unable to work and was confined to his bed with such agonizing pain that the doctors felt compelled to give him unusually large opiates. Much of the time he was delirious and for long periods he had no recollection of what transpired about him. The pain was so bad that doctors said something must be done at once.

After all medicines had failed he was taken to St. Paul Hospital in Dallas. His physician frankly said, "I do not know what is the trouble." Four other good doctors were called in. Their answer was the same. They did not know where the seat of the trouble was that was causing such violent illness and pain, but all agreed that something must be done at once. They decided that the tonsils should be removed. If that did not settle the difficulty, the optic nerve must be clipped. If that did not stop the pain, they would do something else.

The tonsils were removed. Still the illness was not cured. Recovering from the tonsil operation, Mr. Middleton was brought home, and he was still taking regular injections in the arm, was still under the care of the physician.

On a Sunday night, in March, I was called to Brother Middleton's home to pray for him. He was in such pain that he buried his face in the pillow and rolled from side to side, trying to keep control of himself. I had been praying for him for weeks, while I was in the Oklahoma City revival and after I returned. Many members of the church had been praying. But now all the treatments by the doctors had failed, five of them, the best they had known to consult. Brother Middleton had spent two weeks in the hospital.

Anointing With Oil, Following the Bible Command

It seemed time to get the matter settled with God. So there in Brother Middleton's home we agreed that we would do exactly what the Bible said, "pray over him, anointing him with oil in the name of the Lord" according to James 5:14. Mrs. Middleton, Mrs. Rice and I got down on our knees and confessed our sins to each other and to God. We wanted to fulfill every detail of what God commanded. Remember that James 5:14-16 says:

"Is any sick among you? let him call for the elders of the church; and let them pray over him, anointing him with oil in the name of the Lord: And the prayer of faith shall save the sick, and the Lord shall raise him up; and if he have committed sins, they shall be forgiven him. Confess your faults one to another, and pray one for another, that ye may be healed. The effectual fervent prayer of a righteous man availeth much."

After confessing our sins and quoting God's promise, I put my hands upon Brother Middleton's head and prayed that if it would please and honor Him, He would heal Brother Middleton either without any known medicine, without doctors, or with doctors and medicines—just as He chose—but so that everybody would know that God did it, not the doctors. Then Mrs. Middleton prayed, then Mrs. Rice then Brother Middleton. We promised God that if He would heal we would give Him the glory and that we would tell about the anointing with oil as well as the prayer of faith which actually gets the healing.

While we were on our knees, God gave us some faith that He had heard our prayers.

After our prayers, Mrs. Middleton said, "I don't want Mr. Middleton to go back to the doctor tomorrow. If he is willing, we will just trust the Lord and Him alone." Brother Middleton answered, "That is just what we will do." After a time of quiet conversation, Mrs. Rice and I went to our home late that Sunday night.

God Heals

Before we left that night Brother Middleton's pain was a great deal lighter. By the next morning he was better. The next day he did not go back to the doctor. Wednesday came and again he did not keep his appointment with the doctor. The doctor phoned to know why, urging him to come back the next Saturday.

Saturday Brother Middleton went to see the doctor but refused to have an injection in his arm and he had the doctor dismiss his case so he would be free to go back to work.

Brother Middleton had lost twenty-five pounds but he rapidly regained his strength. The following Friday he went back to work. After losing exactly thirty days' work, after a $115.00 doctor bill, after a $150.00 hospital and nurse's bill, losing his tonsils and after almost unbearable pain, God healed Brother Middleton in answer to prayer and following the anointing with oil. I say praise the Lord for answered prayer and for proof that God is just the same, and that the Bible is still up to date!

We promised God to give our testimony and we are doing it here and now so that everybody may be encouraged to call on God in time of sickness or any other time of need. Besides that, I want people to be encouraged to take the Bible literally and follow it literally.

King Asa "Sought Not to the Lord, But to the Physicians

Gathered around that bed of pain Sunday night, March 14, we read II Chronicles 16:12, 13 which says:

"And Asa in the thirty and ninth year of his reign was diseased in his feet, until his disease was exceeding great: yet in his disease he sought not to the Lord, but to the physicians. And Asa slept with his fathers, and died in the one and fortieth year of his reign."

We had prayed but depended on the doctors. We decided not to be like Asa but to depend on the Lord. So we followed the explicit Bible command and prayed for Brother Middleton, anointing him with oil in the name of the Lord.

I have told the above story because it is true and because we promised God to tell it. I do not believe it is always wrong to use medicine and doctors. God can heal with doctors and medicine, or without them. Sometimes He does it one way, sometimes the other. But certainly the modern tendency is to trust the doctors instead of the Lord. I am certain that God ought always to have the credit for the healing, however it comes. I am certain that sometimes He wants to do it without doctors and without medicine. We are all sure in this case that God Himself did the healing and that doctors and medicine had very little or nothing to do with his healing. In any case, God deserves the glory and must have it.

Nor do I believe it is always God's will to heal. The Bible says that "it is appointed unto man once to die," (Heb. 9:27). God did not promise healing except by "the prayer of faith." If God gives the faith, He will do the healing. If God does not give the faith, He may not heal.

Sometimes in His mercy He heals people who do not even pray.

In any case, our duty is clear. God said, "Is any among you afflicted? let him pray" (James 5:13). People who are sick ought to pray. Likewise, James 5:14 says, "Is any sick among you? let him call for the elders of the church; and let them pray over him, anointing him with oil in the name of the Lord." People who are sick and feel the need of it ought to call the elders or preachers and have them pray. Preachers ought to be willing, whenever possible, to do just what the Lord commanded here, that is, to "pray over him, anointing him with oil in the name of the Lord." That is the preacher's part. Then the healing is God's part, if it be His will to give it. We should trust Him if we can. If God gives faith, He will give the healing. Sometimes it is not His will to heal and in such cases He can reveal His will and give grace to bear the sickness to His own glory, as He promised Paul about his thorn in the flesh (II Cor. 12:1-7).

Why Anoint With Oil?

I do not claim that olive oil on a person's head will heal him. The Bible does not so teach. Evidently the oil is to be used as a reminder of the power of the Holy Spirit who dwells in the body of the sick Christian. This Bible command about anointing with oil is evidently not for the unsaved but for God's children. The Holy Spirit dwells in the body of every believer, every born-again child of God (I Cor. 6:19, 20; I Cor. 3:16, 17; I Cor. 12:13; Rom. 8:9). When a Christian sins and grieves the Holy Spirit with his sin, then sickness, or even death may come on a Christian because of his sin (Eph. 4:30). Some of the Corinthian Christians were weak and sickly and some died for this reason (I Cor. 11:30-32).

Therefore, when we pray for the sick or for ourselves we should confess our faults one to another that we may be healed (James 5:16). We should seek to please the Holy Spirit who dwells in our bodies, and then as a recognition of this Holy Spirit's presence and power we anoint the sick with oil. The anointing with oil does not heal the sick. The Holy Spirit does that if it is done.

In New Testament times people were sometimes healed by faith without the anointing with oil, as we are clearly told in Acts 5:15 and 16, Acts 3:1-8 and elsewhere. I believe they had more faith than we do. I know that God has sometimes answered prayer for the sick without anointing with oil. I believe that sometimes the anointing with oil strengthens our faith and helps us definitely to trust the Lord for His healing power.

I want no one to call for me to anoint them with oil and pray, unless he is willing to have a most rigid examination and confession of his sins. I believe sin is back of most sickness (not all). I do not believe that anointing with oil and prayer will heal any one unless God gives the faith. I do not believe God will use these means to heal people living in rebellion and in grievous sin. I am no quack and I want no fame. I am no healer. I am sure I will be pestered by people who want me to pray for them, anointing them with oil, who are not willing to confess their sins, clean up their lives and please God. I am sure that some will think I am a fanatic and a crank and will class me with so-called "divine healers" who oftentimes are not true to the Bible in doctrine and who often claim more than they can do. But that does not deter me. I believe the Bible, and I intend to follow the Bible. Besides that, thank God it works!

As far as that goes, I say frankly that a fanatic who believes the Bible is far better off than the most sensible and well-balanced man who does not believe the Bible, and I am willing to take my stand with all those who believe the Word of God.

Do Not Explain Away the Bible

Unbelief always has a tendency to explain away the Bible. Some say that James 5:14 and 15 are not to be followed today. They say it is not good "Baptist doctrine." Others say it was for Jews only. One great and good man who used to practice anointing with oil and with whom I have joined in that privilege, now says it is only figurative and not to be carried out literally.

I remind you that modernists say that the Genesis account of creation is only figurative and allegorical. I deny it. They say man came by evolution while I say God made man out of the dust of the earth exactly like He said He did.

Modernists say that the story of Jonah and the whale is only a parable, is allegory and that it never really happened. I take it literally. I believe God prepared a great fish (Jesus said it was a whale), and that this fish swallowed Jonah and then after three days and nights cast him out on the land. That is what the Bible says and I believe it. I do not explain it away.

So with the other miracles of the Bible—the virgin birth, the bodily resurrection, the feeding of the five thousand, etc. I believe it is a sin to explain them away. I believe the Bible means what it says. I believe the miracles occurred just like the Bible says they did. Why should Christians explain away the Bible?

Postmillennialists and amillennialists believe that God's covenant with Abraham, whereby the land of Palestine was given to him and his seed for an everlasting possession, will not be literally fulfilled. They do not believe that Christ will literally sit on the throne of David at Jerusalem, like the Bible says. They do not believe that Christ will personally and literally reign on the earth for a thousand years, though the Bible expressly says so. Post-millennialists are great for explaining away the prophecies.

But what is the difference in explaining away the Old Testament prophecies, the bodily return and reign of Christ, and a New Testament command about anointing with oil and praying for the sick? Why explain away either? Why not take both literally, if one is to be taken literally? That is a good question for all fundamentalists who believe in taking the Bible literally, "with nothing added to it and with nothing taken from it, from the first preposition 'in' in Genesis, to the last 'Amen' of Revelation." If part of the Bible is not to be taken at face value, then why take the last of it seriously? Who has the authority to say what part we shall take just like God gave it and what part we shall explain away and say it meant something else?

The Bullingerites, the hyper-dispensationalists, say that baptism, the Lord's Supper, and the Great Commission are not for this age. That makes fundamentalist Baptists tear their hair and I do not blame them. But what is the difference in saying that the command about baptism is not for us and saying that the command about anointing with oil is not for us? One could easily say that baptism is only a symbol anyway, just as you can say that the anointing of oil is only a symbol of the Holy Spirit. If you leave off one command, then why not leave off the other?

But let me put it in a better way. Why leave off either one? Why explain or ignore anything that the Word of God plainly says? Who has a right to say that one New Testament command is important and that another New Testament command is not important? I do not say that anointing with oil has as prominent a place in the New Testament as baptism does, but I do say that both are in the New Testament alike, that both are for this age alike and that one command is as clear as the other.

The Lesson for Us Today

The lesson I want to get home to every Christian is this: First, there is a God in Heaven who answers prayer and does it today just the same as He did in Bible times. Second, the Bible is a safe rule and the only safe rule for New Testament Christians to follow. It should be taken literally, at face value, and followed in simple faith and with an obedient heart, trusting God to answer.

And let all the objectors take note of this one fact that cannot be gainsaid.

Today, in answer to the prayer of faith, Mr. J. A. Middleton is back at work, strong, healthy, and happy. After doctors, medicines, hospitals, nurses, and other

human agencies had absolutely failed, after spending about
$300, losing about thirty days of work, and going through
terrible pain, God heard our prayers when we anointed
with oil, just like He said, when up to that time He
certainly had not given the answer. Say what you will, that
is a fact that can be verified and no one can deny it. God
alone deserves the credit and He shall have it.

Brother Middleton has been so happy and has gotten
such a spiritual blessing in His healing, that he has been
winning souls every day and has brought in the names of
seventeen people, most of them men, who have claimed
Christ as Saviour in his personal work since he was raised
up from his sickness a few days ago! Some of them are
white men, some of them are colored. Some of them have
been truly remarkable conversions. One was a man who
claimed to be an infidel! Brother Middleton himself does
not doubt the reality of a God who answers prayers and a
Bible that is good for 1935 the same as it was in the days of
the apostles.

A Personal Testimony by J. A. Middleton

"I have read Brother Rice's article above, and I want
to say that it is true and I want to give God the glory for
healing me.

"I want to say, too, that since the Lord healed me in
answer to prayer, I have had more power in soul
winning than I ever had before.

"I want to praise the Lord that we have a pastor that
believes in praying for the sick like Brother Rice does.

"I want to thank all the membership and all the
friends for their prayers during my sickness.

(Signed) "J. A. Middleton"

8.
SOUL-WINNING JOY FOR CHRISTIANS

CONSIDER THESE WONDERFUL FACTS ABOUT SOUL WINNING:

It Is the Way Most Are Won

A famous preacher said he had preached for years to great congregations, for twenty years had written weekly to a religious paper which had, some of the time, a circulation of 100,000 copies, and was the author of thirty books, but that in this time he had won more people to Christ in private conversation than in sermon, or print, as far as he knew. The late Dr. A. C. Dixon said the same thing.

Some preachers think that the public expounding of the Word to crowds is the main thing. Not so. Preaching the Gospel is the main thing, and every Christian can do that with one hearer. Great preachers must be great personal soul winners. I know a girl who won three times as many souls last year as was won in the whole ministry of the average Southern Baptist preacher, with all the help he had from his workers, according to the Southern Baptist Handbook. And those who are saved in public service without private help are few.

Every Christian Can Do It

Yes, every Christian can win souls if he will pay the price. The Bible does not leave the preaching to preachers. Deacons also preached in public. John 15 is to every Christian. Matthew 28:19, 20 is to all. It doesn't take worldly wisdom, nor gift of speech, nor special training. It just takes a broken heart and Holy Spirit power, thank God!

It can be done anywhere. I have seen people saved in church, at home, by a well, two in an orchard and at least twenty by the roadside, some in my car, one on an interurban car, several in hospitals, scores in jails, one walking down Main Street in Fort Worth, one on the top of a barn, even one Methodist at a baptizing! I have seen them saved in a crowd or alone. Mothers, fathers, brother, sister, sweethearts, teachers, and rank strangers can win them. Sometimes just tears will decide it. More often a verse of Scripture. Many, many times just the touch of a hand turns a man to Christ. All can win souls.

It Costs Something

A woman once said to an evangelist, "Oh, I would give the world if I could win souls as you do!" "That's just what it cost me," answered the soul winner.

Soul winning costs something. It cannot be done best and the most effective without deep knowledge of God's word and experience. It cannot be done at all without surrender to God and Holy Spirit leadership.

It costs time, tears, labor and sacrifice to become an artist, and soul winning is the finest of arts. Thank God, this is the one artistic possibility born in us all, but at the second birthday. Great soul winners are men of burdened hearts, single purpose, secret vigil, and unreserved surrender. Oh, it costs! It cost Jesus Bethlehem and Gethsemane and Calvary—betrayal and blood, torture and tears. It costs, but, thank God, it pays more than it costs.

It Is Contagious

One example is worth a thousand arguments. Let a fellow try this blessed business of winning souls, and let others see that people want to be saved, see that it is not natural ability but Holy Spirit leadership and humble surrender to God that gets results, and they will try it. The way to learn to preach is to preach, and the way to learn to win souls is to get at it.

How preachers should set the holy example of personal approach to individuals. How we should hold up the personal work of Jesus and of Paul, His great apostle. How we should pray for an irresistible epidemic of individuals seeking individuals, like that which we have often seen in modern times in Wales and in other places. It will take time and teaching, but above all, it will take examples—examples from the ministry especially, but also from the ranks of business men, women, and young people to start a revival of personal seeking and winning the lost in private and in public services outside the pulpit. Soul winning is contagious.

It Will Keep the Christian Right

The monks who spent their days in prayer and self-affliction were not near to God's heart and plan. A preacher who preaches to crowds and lives in pleasant places among generous and kindly people, is often not right with God, nor happy, nor victorious. I know. I have been there. But the man who has had the continuous evidence of

God's blessing on his ministry in personally winning the lost, may be sure he is on the right track.

How often I have tried to preach when words were hollow, the sky was brass, and weighty words went from a cold heart to colder ears. How often the Book had no message, and there was no joy in prayer. How often the weight of a service was breaking my heart and I had no victory for the sermon. Then I have slipped away to a neighbor, or more often among boys and girls, and privately sought the appointed one with the hungry heart, and told him again the sweet story that lived again in my heart with the telling, saw tears flow, heard the great confession, felt the angels rejoicing again. Then I have gone again to public ministry and found that the Holy One had taken an ember from dead ashes in my heart, lighted a coal from the Book of God and fanned it with His Heavenly presence to a holy blessed flame. O brethren, personal, earnest, heartbroken seeking of the lost by us preachers, not as preachers but as Christians, will fix our ministries, will fix our temptations, will fix our prayers, as nothing else will, because God will see to it that we can win souls only in proportion as we are right. Soul winning both gains and proves the abiding Holy Spirit.

Young Christian, what about worldly amusements? Is it hard to give them up? Soul winning will take away their charm. Do you have trouble remembering prayer? Get a sinning, hopeless, hungry, lost world on your heart, and go fishing for men with tears, and you cannot help praying. Soul winning will keep the Christian right.

It Is the Highest Joy

"They that sow in tears shall reap in joy." A Christian's best joy does not come when he is saved but when he helps some one else to the Saviour. The soul winner has the joy of God's favor, of the saved one's gratitude, and the Holy Spirit's abiding. Clothes wear out, money disappears, land doesn't go to Heaven, a night of pleasure is gone in the morning; but souls won will be in Heaven to meet us and to shine "as the stars forever and forever."

Christians, the personal seeking, wooing winning of Christ's lost sheep is God's balm of Gilead to restless, worrying, unhappy hearts. To win souls is the greatest glory to Jesus, the greatest gain in Heaven, the greatest growth to the soul winner, and the highest joy on earth.

Why not right now, before you lay this book down, open your heart and ask God to make you a compassionate winner of lost men. Nothing else on earth pays in such coin.

9.
THE GREATEST JOY—GOD ALWAYS WITH US

"Let your conversation be without covetousness; and be content with such things as ye have: for he hath said, I will never leave thee, nor forsake thee. So that we may boldly say, The Lord is my helper, and I will not fear what man shall do unto me."—Heb. 13:5, 6.

"I will never leave thee, nor forsake thee" is a quotation from Deuteronomy. Then, "The Lord is my helper, and I will not fear what man shall do unto me" is a quotation from the Psalms. We can say that God never leaves His own alone.

First, consider the great eternal fact of salvation. God is with us, with the Holy Spirit dwelling in our bodies. The Spirit of God dwells in you. "What? know ye not that your body is the temple of the Holy Ghost which is in you, which ye have of God, and ye are not your own? For ye are bought with a price" (I Cor. 6:19, 20). The eternal fact of salvation is that the Holy Spirit who came in to regenerate you now lives in your body. And the Holy Spirit manifests God the Father and God the Son, living in your body.

Second, God is with us in a God-like new nature. I can say like Paul, "So then with the mind I myself serve the law of God." I can say that we are partakers of the divine nature. And God lives in us in the sense that a father lives in his son, or a mother lives in a child; in the sense we become absolutely part of God, actually, literally children of God, partakers of His nature. So there is the eternal fact of salvation.

That means also in the sense that Jesus is our High Priest and ever lives to intercede for us, according to the will of God. "Wherefore he is able also to save them to the uttermost that come unto God by him." I say, there are certain great facts of salvation involving the Lord Jesus who is with us always and who never leaves us alone.

Jesus Personally With His Own

But there is something better than that, which I want to teach here. In a very intimate, sweet, loving, wooing way the Lord is with us. He gave the Great Commission in Matthew 28:19, 20: "Go ye therefore, and teach all nations, baptizing them in the name of the Father, and of the Son, and of the Holy Ghost: Teaching them to observe all things whatsoever I have commanded you: and, lo, I am with you alway, even unto the end of the world." Notice He said, "Lo, I am with you alway." I think there He does not mean only that He is in you in the Holy Spirit, nor that we have now the nature of God and can now go our way. I think He does not primarily mean even that Jesus says, "I am standing at the right hand of the Father and interceding for you." No, Jesus said that in some way you could feel it, enjoy it, be comforted with it, and that you can have a daily fellowship with Him. He said, "Lo, I am with you alway."

So one who is in the will of God can be conscious of the Lord's constant fellowship. He can know His sweet peace, like holding the hand of a friend in the dark; like reaching over at night and feeling the face of your wife by your side; like the little one who reaches out to feel if Daddy is there. I say, one can feel God's presence all the time.

That is true about the psalmist. In Psalm 139 David said, beginning with verse 7:

"Whither shall I go from thy spirit? or whither shall I flee from thy presence? If I ascend up into heaven, thou art there: if I make my bed in hell, behold, thou art there. If I take the wings of the morning, and dwell in the uttermost parts of the sea; Even there shall thy hand lead me, and thy right hand shall hold me. If I say, Surely the darkness shall cover me; even the night shall be light about me. Yea, the darkness hideth not from thee; but the night shineth as the day: the darkness and the light are both alike to thee."

The Testimony of Dr. Held

God is with you in the dark. You cannot see Him, but He is there. You can't feel Him, but He is there.

I had a friend, Dr. John A. Held, who was the editor of *The Gulf Coast Baptist*, the Southern Baptist paper down in Houston, Texas. He was a widely used good man of God. His daughter was in my class at Baylor University. Now he has gone to Heaven. In 1951 I saw in *The Gulf Coast Baptist* this editorial by Dr. Held:

Until recently, this editor has experienced mental agony and sleepless nights for many months. It seemed that everything went wrong. We were inclined to hesitate on almost everything. Our faith became weak and our courage was at the lowest level. Then it was I received the book for review from John R. Rice, *God's Cure for Anxious Care*. We reviewed it and were impressed in our hurried reading of it. Nevertheless, we felt it was a book worth reading again.

When we were under the greatest strain and did not know which way to turn, we picked up the book again.

This time we read it with great care. We were especially impressed with the correctness and scripturalness. Looking up every reference, we read every word carefully. Not because we had never read the words before, but because in our stress we came to see what we had not seen before, namely that God really made certain promises and with such clarity and assurance that it is amazing why anyone should not accept these promises for their full worth. Then came the answer with freshness and such definiteness that we once again accepted those precious words with the assurance of certainty and found a new joy.

Since then we have had much joy and blessed satisfaction by leaning on these promises, and resting our souls on what He had said.

The trouble is that many of our prayers are not honest to God. Many of us have had the audacity to ask our Heavenly Father to hand out blessings that we do not deserve.

Somewhere we read the story recently about the great sorrow and heartbroken condition of a great businessman. One evening he was so distressed that he cried out, more to himself rather than to the family in the room, "I have suffered and endured great mental strain and now I have lost everything." Then the daughter, evidently sympathizing with her father and taking things literally, said, "Daddy, you have me and Mommy yet." What a rebuke!

The other day I turned once again to the Psalm and for the thousandth time read, "The Lord is my shepherd; I shall not want." I said to myself, "Have I forgotten His blessed Word?"

God Is With You, Whether You Feel His Presence or Not

I am again reading from an editorial by Dr. John A.

Held in *The Gulf Coast Baptist,* February 1, 1951:

> But again John Rice writes a wise word and one that has tremendous meaning when he says, "This matter of God's presence with His people is not for a favored few, but for all, every born-again child of God can know that God is with him. He has promised ever to be with him and never to forsake him. On this matter we are not to go by our feelings. God is with you when you feel His presence. But He is also with you when you do not feel His presence. God is with you when your heart is happy, when your faith is high. He is also with you when you are downcast and discouraged and unbelieving."
>
> That is as fine a word as ever uttered by the greatest saints, both in the pulpit and out of it. Thank God for His unspeakable gift! Thank God for His unfailing promises. Thank God for His lifting power and guiding force in the hearts and lives of people everywhere and at all times.

*   *   *

Here it is, "I will never leave thee, nor forsake thee." Do you believe that? That good man was comforted by the little book, *God's Cure for Anxious Care.*

I call your attention again to the blessed Scripture in Hebrews 13:5 and 6: "Let your conversation be without covetousness; and be content with such things as ye have: for he hath said, I will never leave thee, nor forsake thee. So that we may boldly say, The Lord is my helper, and I will not fear what man shall do unto me."

Jacob Found, With Surprise, "God Is in This Place and I Knew It Not"

Listen friend, a Christian can have peace. God is with

you. He will never leave you. Jacob found that out when he was a lonely boy running away from home, running from the hatred of his brother Esau who would kill him; running from his conscience too, for he lied to his old father and deceived him, and had cheated to gain the birthright. Jacob learned that when he came to a lonely place at Luz and when the night came on and there was no inn, a rock became his pillow. I guess he had no money to buy a bed had there been an inn. He lay down and went to sleep.

In the night he saw a vision and a ladder was erected on earth which reached to Heaven. He saw the angels of God and God appeared and said, "I will be with you like I was with Abraham and Isaac. I will give you this land."

Jacob awoke and said, "God was in this place and I knew it not." God is there where you are—in your room, in your chair, in your bed, in your car, in your office, whether you know it or not.

No Need for Covetousness Then

God never leaves nor forsakes His own. There is no need for covetousness because if you have Christ, you have everything. "Let your conversation be without covetousness; and be content with such things as ye have: for he hath said, I will never leave thee, nor forsake thee." The Bible says we are heirs with God and joint heirs with Christ. All things are yours, Paul says. Thank God, one day we will inherit all things.

God cares for the flowers, and even Solomon in all his glory was not arrayed like one of these. God clothed them. O ye of little faith! God looks after His own.

Consider the birds. Not a sparrow falls to the ground without your Father. They do not gather in the barns, yet your Heavenly Father feeds them. Then wouldn't God care for His own? We have no need for covetousness.

> Why should I charge my soul with care?
> The wealth of every mine belongs to Christ, God's Son
>   and heir.
> And He is a friend of mine.

Thank God, we have Jesus, and He never leaves us alone!

Then we don't have any fear of the future. "I shall not fear what man shall do unto me." We may boldly say that, the Scripture says. Why should we have to fear, when God has promised to never leave us alone? Poverty? He will be with us in poverty. There will be no poverty unless it is the will of God. War? Not unless God permits it for His own purposes. Failure? There can be none in the perfect will of God. So let us say, "I will trust the Lord. I will be done with fear."

Don't be afraid to go anywhere Jesus leads. You will never be alone. Don't be afraid of any danger. Livingstone went across Africa and he said, "I have the word of a perfect gentleman who never breaks His word. He said, 'Lo, I am with you alway.'" And so Livingstone was as safe in Africa in the will of God as he would have been back in England. Elijah was safe even if Jezebel swore he would die by tomorrow night. He was as safe as if all the king's armies were protecting him. God was with him. The dungeon is freedom if God is there. Poverty really means riches if one but realizes his wealth in the continual presence of God.

The Christian who realizes this truth is ready for all the darts that Satan can hurl; ready for the darkest night of sorrow that can ever come. There is no need to fret about provisions, but rather "be content with such things as ye have: for he hath said, I will never leave thee, nor forsake thee." Do not be afraid of men, do not be afraid of war, do not be afraid of the atomic bomb. We may boldly say, "The

Lord is my helper, and I will not fear what man shall do unto me."

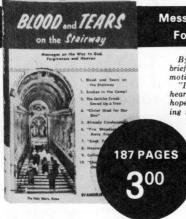

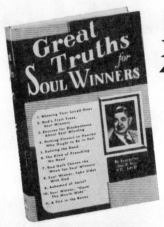